Mother
IN THE
Middle

MOTHER
IN THE
MIDDLE

Searching for Peace
in the
Mommy Wars

DEBORAH SHAW LEWIS &
CHARMAINE CROUSE YOEST

ZondervanPublishingHouse
Grand Rapids, Michigan

A Division of HarperCollinsPublishers

Mother in the Middle
Copyright © 1996 by Deborah Shaw Lewis and Charmaine Yoest

Requests for information should be addressed to:

ZondervanPublishingHouse
Grand Rapids, Michigan 49530

Library of Congress Cataloging-in-Publication Data

Lewis, Deborah Shaw, 1951–
    Mother in the middle : searching for peace in the mommy wars / Deborah
Shaw Lewis and Charmaine Crouse Yoest.
       p. cm.
    Includes bibliographical references.
    ISBN 0-310-20692-8 (softcover)
    1. Mothers—United States—Social conditions.   2. Motherhood—United
States.   3. Working mothers—United States.   4. Work and family—United
States.   5. Mother and child—United States.   I. Yoest, Charmaine Crouse,
1964– . II. Title.
HQ759.L4854   1996
306.874'3—dc20   96-10549
CIP

Edited by Robin Schmitt
Interior design by Sherri L. Hoffman

Printed in the United States of America

96 97 98 99 00 01 02 /❖ DH/ 10 9 8 7 6 5 4 3 2 1

"The Lord . . . lifts up; he humbles and he exalts."
HANNAH'S PRAYER, 1 SAMUEL 2: 6–7

For our daughters
Sarah Lisette and Hannah Ruth
With Love,
May you grow to become wise women.

Contents

PART III: Searching for Peace

A Personal Introduction—
The Women We Are

Who is the Mother in the Middle? She is any woman struggling to meet the often conflicting needs of her family, her children, her work, and herself. Even in this post-superwoman age, when many of us are beginning to realize that we can't have it all—or at least, not all at once—we still expect mothers to be too many things to too many people, all at the same time. The mother in the middle is pulled in so many different directions; she is living with a divided heart.

You will meet many such mothers in these pages: from Madison Avenue executives to small-town factory shift-workers, from successful entrepreneurs to Kmart clerks. On the surface, they don't have much in common. But we found, as we talked to women all across this nation, from all different walks of life, that they had very similar struggles. They were all searching for peace.

We too don't appear to have much in common. As authors, we will speak with one voice throughout most of this book. Yet we are very different women who brought two distinct and varied life experiences to this project.

Deborah grew up in the fifties and sixties. Charmaine came of age during the seventies and eighties. We speak as members of two different generations.

Raised in small-town Georgia, Deborah is a born-and-bred southerner. Charmaine's family lived in the Midwest, the Northeast, and even overseas. For all of her adult life, she's worked and resided in the metropolitan Washington, D.C., area. So we've seen the world from two different perspectives.

Deborah's area of expertise is early childhood education. She received her master's degree from the Erikson Institute in Chicago and has spent over twenty years in her field, writing curriculum, directing day care, nursery school, and mother's-morning-out programs, teaching college, and (what she loves best) working with small children in a wide variety of settings.

Charmaine's career has been focused on the policy side. She has researched and written about national family-policy issues and been a national figure in the pro-family debate, speaking to the media and lobbying and testifying on Capitol Hill. She is also pursuing her doctorate in government at the University of Virginia. So we come from different careers.

A conservative through and through, Charmaine's first job out of college put her political idealism into practice as she served in the Reagan White House. Deborah could never bring herself to vote for a Republican presidential candidate, even when her own sister was one of his speechwriters. So we don't always share the same political agenda.

It's probably no surprise, then, that we've approached motherhood from two different directions, bringing with us two different sets of expectations. Since we're going to tell you the stories of many different women in this book, let us begin by telling you ours.

Deborah

I always knew that I wanted to have children. I do not remember ever making that choice. I just knew.

When I fell in love with my husband, Gregg, in college and we discussed a family, I always told him I wanted twenty-five children. I was only half joking.

By the time we got married, we had settled on three children and thought it would be wise to wait several years to have them.

Four and a half years later we decided it was time to try to get pregnant. After a year, we wondered what was wrong. We saw the first in a long series of doctors. We became familiar with a wide variety of medical tests that intruded into our intimate lives. I took my basal body temperature every morning and recorded it on special graphs. We checked out every book on the topic from every library we had access to.

And every month I wasn't pregnant, I grieved.

Before, when I had thought about children, when we had talked about a family, I had known, with my intellect, that motherhood was an experience I did not want to miss. Now, each month that I did not get pregnant, I felt the loss on a deep, emotional level. I hadn't known how important having children was to me.

My longing for a baby was like an intense personal hunger that nothing else could fill. On more than one occasion, I left doctors' offices and wept with an intensity I had never known before.

Complicating our infertility problems was my career. I had graduated with a B.A. in elementary education. Afterward I had taken a job at a day-care center, teaching three-year-olds. That center was the worst that child care can be—you will learn more about it in chapter 7—but I fell in love with preschoolers.

Several years later I took the position of director at a Winkie Bear Child Development Center. My school was one of a small chain of day-care centers in and around Chicago known for their dedication to providing quality child care. I am proud, even today, to be able to say that I was part of the Winkie Bear Schools. We were the best that private day care could offer.

But as I saw children I loved going in and out of those doors each day, I knew I could never put a child of mine in any day care, even one as good as my Winkie Bear School.

By the completion of my third year as director of Winkie Bear, we had learned that I had several fertility problems. Two different fertility specialists informed us that we would probably never have children.

My emotional frame of mind at the time made it very difficult for me to continue to work in day care. At my center, I saw children coming and going each day who were hungry for their mothers' time and attention, in somewhat the same way I was hungry for a baby. I would have loved to have taken any one of them home with me.

Instead, I resigned to start my graduate work in early childhood education, at the Erikson Institute in Chicago. And in early December we received the best news I think I have ever heard. I was pregnant. Our doctor called it a "miracle." We considered it a gift from God.

Nothing, not even the emotional turmoil of our infertility experience, prepared me for the intensity of childbirth. Holding our son, Andrew, to my breast, looking into his eyes, was exhilarating, earth shattering, life changing, empowering. The way in which I viewed life was forever altered.

Eighteen months later we had a second miracle: Matthew. To my astonishment, his birth was just as exhilarating, life changing, incredible.

And our lives filled up with miracles: two and a half years later Lisette joined our lives. Nineteen months after that, Benjamin surprised us by coming nine days early. Jonathan came along three years after Benjamin. And with each child came joy, tears, laughter, incredible strength, and a life of rich texture and variety. No two of them are alike. Each brings individual style and personality into our family mix. Each has enriched my life beyond measure. I cannot imagine my life without any one of them.

I had not known how much joy children would bring to my life. No one ever told me how hard or how stressful the work of mothering would be. But I count my children as first on my list of blessings.

Charmaine

Unlike Debi, I never had much interest in being a mom. Looking back, my husband, Jack, and I both marvel; neither of us were very interested in babies and children—they just weren't on our radar screen.

I did want children. That, however, is very different from wanting to be a mother.

I'm part of the career generation, and I soaked up all the superwoman messages like a sponge. Career was the thing. And by the time I became pregnant, mine was going very well. Beyond my dreams, even.

So even when I was pregnant, I still wasn't all that eager to become a mom. I was excited about the baby, sure. But not about the mom thing. And I wasn't having one of those glorious, bonding pregnancies; I felt miserable all the time. I had thought morning sickness meant morning, not all day!

I didn't want to leave my job: when I was seven months pregnant, I appeared on *The Sally Jesse Raphael Show;* at eight months, I was part of a panel discussion featured in *Good Housekeeping;* and three weeks before delivery, I appeared on *CBS This Morning.* I was working hard to prove to my co-workers that I was still the same professional and that nothing had changed. I didn't even have the nursery ready for the baby.

But at home, Jack and I were having long, agonized discussions about my life. These talks were liberally baptized with my tears. My whole existence had been geared toward advancing professionally, and I had driven so hard. But while working in family policy, I had read the data on infant attachment; I had seen the research on day care; I had learned how critical a mother's presence was to babies. I didn't want to leave my job, but intellectually I didn't see any way around it. As I lurched toward the most major transition of my life, resigning my position was strictly a head decision—I sure didn't feel it in my heart.

And then . . . there was Hannah. She was here.

Suddenly, unbelievably, being with her had nothing to do with research. My friends remind me that I just kept saying, "I can't imagine my life without her." For the first few weeks, I lived in sheer terror that something might happen to her that I could have prevented. Now it was all heart: no one, no thing, was going to come between me and my baby.

It hasn't been easy. I still remember the first time a former coworker referred glibly to a piece of legislation, pending on Capitol Hill, by an acronym, expecting that I would know what he was talking about. I did not. And suddenly I felt terribly out of touch.

But my decision was made; my course was set. Because I had decided in my head, fully expecting motherhood to be a difficult (at best) experience, I was set free to be surprised by joy in my heart. As I think back over the last two and a half years, some of my favorite memories are the worst ones: up all night with a sick, confused toddler who is throwing up every hour; waking up in the middle of the night to find that I'm sitting on the living room couch and holding a sleeping newborn, tired and disoriented and not remembering how and when I got there.

It's funny to think of finding peace in a house with a toddler and a crawling baby. Nevertheless, I have found mine. . . . Maybe that's because peace is such a close cousin to joy. That we have in abundance.

In the midst of all that divides us and makes the two of us different, we found to our surprise much to agree upon, much about motherhood that we share in common.

We are both mothers in the middle.

We have lived what we write about here. Between us, we have seven children, ranging from nine months to sixteen years of age. In the chaos of writing this book, they have served to remind us about and reinforce for us the importance of motherhood.

And the challenge. As our deadline loomed, Debi's son Matthew required oral surgery, and she coped with the scheduling challenge of having four children playing on (and practicing with) four different basketball teams in one season. Both of Charmaine's children simultaneously came down with their first-ever ear infections.

They needed us. As the mother of the two youngest children, Charmaine in particular had child care difficulties. The first baby-sitter left suddenly after two months, just as the children were settling into a routine. As the next baby-sitter tried to get to know Hannah, a spirited two-and-a-half-year-old, and John, a cheerful six-month-old, Charmaine had an experience that crystallized for us the struggle of the mother in the middle:

It had been a crazy morning, and at ten o'clock I was still in my bathrobe. I felt like a caricature of myself—the only thing that made me feel remotely like a professional was the impending chapter deadline looming in front of me. I had to get some work done.

The baby-sitter had the children in their coats, and they were happily headed outside to play. I heaved a sigh of relief and headed for the shower. Hannah started to balk. "No! You come, too, Mommy!" she cried. "You push the stroller."

My heart seized up. Was this a discipline problem, or did she need attention? I chose the former. "Hannah," I said firmly, "you go outside and play." And I got in the shower.

Through two closed doors and splashing water, I could hear two-and-a-half-year-old Armageddon. Bewildered, John joined in, and my poor new baby-sitter was in way over her head.

Dripping and furious, I climbed out of the shower. Tears streaming down her face, Hannah bodily threw herself at me and locked her arms around my neck. I knew in my heart that this wasn't about discipline. This was need. I just didn't want to face it. I had deadlines pending.

"Hannah," I said gently, "Mommy has work to do. I want you to have fun—you go outside and have fun playing. It would be boring for you in Mommy's office."

"Mommy," she whispered, almost inaudibly, "I want to go to you boring office."

And for much of that day, that's precisely where she was—under the computer table, happily cutting up papers.

This project was intensely personal; we too have struggled with the issues we'll talk about. In the process, we've come to believe that today's debate has lost sight of this essential truth: our children need us.

As we talked with the mothers in the middle, we laughed with them—and we cried. We despaired at times, but we were also inspired. We want to share those stories with you. We come away from this project with great hope. We believe there is common ground.

Perhaps our own journey to common ground was a little easier, because we are family: Charmaine's mother is Deborah's oldest sister. So Charmaine is Deborah's niece. Nevertheless, we saw the thing that brought us together reflected again and again and again in our discussions with the mothers who shared with us their joys, struggles, fears, and hopes: most mothers in the middle, even while feeling pulled in many different directions, want the best for their children.

We do not believe that society today is helping us in that quest. Indeed, we'll talk about ways in which the Mommy Wars are making it difficult—in some cases, nearly impossible—for the mother in the middle to make the best decisions for her children.

Yet we believe there is peace to be found. There is peace in the mommy wars. But far, far more importantly, there is personal peace for the mother in the middle.

Please, come along with us on our search.

Prologue—
The Voices We Hear

Victoria is on the fast track. As the regional operations director of a national retail chain, she supervises more than ten thousand employees. She is also the mother of an eight-year-old son and a six-year-old daughter—and she works six days a week, traveling overnight at least twice a month to oversee branch operations. She left her last job because it didn't allow for enough family time. Afterward, even though she chose from among nine different job offers, looking for a more balanced lifestyle, her talent keeps propelling her upward. Now she's right back where she started from: her children are in an after-school program until 6:00 every night.

When we asked this thirty-something rising corporate star what the words "mother in the middle" meant to her, she told us:

"That pretty much describes the last nine years of my life. I've not had a day since my son was born that there wasn't some sense of guilt associated, wherever I've been. At work it's, *Gee, I should be with the kids!* (Especially if I'm working late.) If I'm with the kids and I have a pending deadline, it's like, *I'm going to have to stay up until two in the morning, and I'm going to be crabby all day tomorrow!* Those kinds of feelings tear you apart.

"As a mother, it's almost as if you have a black line going down the middle of your body—if you are totally a professional person and you also want to be an outstanding parent and do want your children to be a priority. It's very, very difficult to get that struggle settled. I feel as if I walk around with a black line between 'me.'

"At times I think I have the best of both worlds, but at other times I feel that I have neither. It's very difficult to *have it all*. From what I see, my kids are very well adjusted, yet I also know they crave me more than I'm there for them. I don't want them to look back when they become adults, and have some sort of resentment that I wasn't there for them. Neither do I want to feel that I missed out on everything there was to enjoy about them. I do miss more than I would like to with them."

I feel as if I walk around with a black line between "me."

Victoria is the mother in the middle.

Maria and Jeff, both teachers in their mid-twenties, had been married about two years and were expecting their first child. One day, in a conversation with an older relative about what she planned to do when the baby was born, Maria said, "Jeff says he would like me to stay home and take care of the baby. I think that's really sweet. Old-fashioned, but sweet."

However, she said, her plan was to find "a good day-care home" for the baby and go back to her teaching job when the baby was six weeks old. And that's what she did.

But leaving her daughter, even with a lady from their church that they trusted, proved a lot harder than Maria had ever dreamed. Her little girl, Rebecca, was a year and a half old when her son, Chad, was born. Again Maria went back to her high school teaching position when her six weeks of unpaid leave ended.

She wondered why no one ever told her it would be like this. The intensity of her maternal instincts, this desperate longing to be home with her young children, caught Maria completely by surprise. Almost a year later she left teaching to begin a home-based business she hopes will earn enough money to enable her to stay home with her children.

Business has been slow. Money is tight.

Maria too is the mother in the middle.

Ellen, who is married to a nationally known broadcast executive, is a talented interior designer. Her husband's career has taken them all over the world, and because of the incredible demands of his profession, she has always chosen to maintain her flexibility by working on her own and running her business out of their home, even before they had children. Nevertheless, as in Victoria's case, Ellen's talent kept her in high demand. She was always very busy, even when she and her family lived overseas.

Having her first baby didn't slow her down much. Her son came two weeks early and caught her in the middle of several projects. "When Joseph was born," said Ellen, "I was downstairs at three in the morning, in labor, finishing up work—and a couple days after, back at it again and basically finishing up projects. I never really took any time off."

They continued at breakneck pace for several years and had two more children. And even though things were "crazy" a lot, particularly while her husband was assigned to the White House and traveling almost weekly, it seemed to be working.

However, as her husband's hours grew less and less predictable and flexible, she began carrying more and more of the weight at home. Eventually the pace started to take its toll on Ellen. "Even though I would say that my priorities were our life and our children," she explained, "the priorities really were the customer and the client."

Finally, when her youngest daughter was three years old, Ellen cut back the number of clients she took on, until she was working almost part-time, then later put her business on hold indefinitely.

As Ellen explained it, "It was . . . I got to a point where I think the kids just . . . there was just so much . . ." And her voice trailed off.

Having made the decision, she felt a sense of relief. But it wasn't easy—she had to recreate her identity.

"There was a struggle of not working anymore. I think it was more the idea of: I have my own business and I'm working and I'm doing this. I think it was more the idea of giving that up versus the actual tasks I was doing day to day.

"I have sort of mixed feelings. . . . I've never envisioned myself as a PTA mom . . . probably still don't, even though I'm doing more of that. . . . I had always worked and always thought I would and always thought of that as my part of the family contribution.

"I would say there's a lot of conflict: not just me directly but me along with every other woman I know. . . . I think it's harder in a lot of ways than it was when it was acceptable and respected to be at home and be a mother. You have a lot more choices, which I think is wonderful and necessary, but I think it doesn't always make it easier. Because in some ways, you're not quite there if you're not working; you're missing something if you're not a professional person, and yet you're frustrated if you are. You can't win either way."

Allison and Liz don't know each other. Even if they did, it's not likely they would ever be friends, because they seem to have so little in common. And yet . . .

Allison worked her way up to become the national public relations director of her firm by the time she reached her early thirties. Having her first child never slowed her down; she simply hired a nanny. But when her second child was born, Allison wanted more involvement in her children's lives and worked out a part-time arrangement with her company. The nanny became more of a housekeeper and helper as Allison took over most of the care of her children. When her third child was born, Allison felt even more of a pinch. On the one hand, the responsibilities of mothering three preschoolers didn't allow either time or energy for even a part-time corporate office job. And on the other hand, Allison and her husband, Paul, decided that the birth of their third child necessitated a move from their urban apartment to a much larger—and consequently much more expensive—suburban home. To afford the move, they needed Allison's income more than ever.

The solution they came to was for Allison to resign her job and use her contacts to begin a public relations consulting firm based in her own home. She could be there with and for her kids, develop her career, and bring in the necessary income all at once. The plan worked—almost too well. The consulting business took off. Allison soon had so many clients, she had to hire household help again. But still her role as mother (which she loved) took up so much time that most of her other work had to be done after the kids were in bed at night. Which meant she'd often be up late into the night trying to design creative PR campaigns.

But as any mother of young children knows, even that time wasn't always "free." "I would be up in the middle of the night," Allison told us, "and they were still waking up in the middle of the night."

That's when it all started to be too much. "At this point, I started having a nervous breakdown . . . so to speak," said Allison. "I didn't have a nervous breakdown, but I can say maybe I came close."

Soon Allison and Paul were reaching for a lifestyle change. "I wasn't happy," explained Allison. "It was a very stressful time in our lives. It was wild. But I couldn't slow down, because of the expense of living in our area and this house that we had moved into."

Then there is Liz and her husband, Arnie, both factory workers in a north Georgia paper mill. They had a seven-year-old son when their daughter was born last year. Though her six weeks of unpaid leave presented a real financial hardship to their family, Liz cherished every moment of her time with the little girl she'd dreamed of having for years. She told Arnie she didn't want to go back to work. Arnie insisted they had no choice. He saw no way to support a family of four on the pay of one unskilled factory worker. They needed both incomes.

The only feasible plan, because day care costs for a newborn would eat up most of Liz's hourly wage, was for the two of them to work different shifts. Since Liz wanted to have as much time as possible with her newborn daughter, she opted to be home during the day and work the midnight shift at the paper mill. Arnie would be home to care for the kids at night and work a regular day shift at the mill.

A few days into this schedule, a friend spotted Liz carrying her daughter and walking her son down the school hall to his second-grade class at 8:15 in the morning. "How's it going with your little one, Liz?" the friend asked.

"Horrible!" Liz admitted. "I cry every night when I have to leave her to go to work. She cries half the night. Arnie cries. We all cry. And none of us are getting enough sleep."

Liz and Allison are both mothers in the middle.

Kathy stood and watched Kendra, her youngest child, march off toward kindergarten and wished she could share her daughter's excitement at the first day of school. Instead, she felt something dying inside. Where had the time gone?

Kathy held a good secretarial job for the local school board. She and her husband, Al, had lived comfortably, though not extravagantly, on their two incomes for several years before their son, William, was born. To maintain their lifestyle, they both agreed that Kathy would return to work when William was six weeks old and Al's mother could care for the baby.

That's when the "somedays" began. Kathy's heart was torn with the longing to be home. *Someday*, she kept hoping, *maybe we can afford that.*

When Kendra arrived, Al argued that with a larger family, they needed her income and benefits more than ever. So Kathy kept working. And kept hoping.

She had been cherishing the dream of staying home with her children for nine years. Now she was watching that hope die as Kendra turned and waved before disappearing through the door of her kindergarten class.

The death of Kathy's dream brought a very real yet unrecognized grief that turned into a "mysterious" depression that fall; Kathy went into a long, dark, emotionally unpredictable period. "Someday" had never come.

Kathy is also the mother in the middle.

Peggy is a pharmacist, a mother of three, who has worked either full-time or part-time since her oldest daughter was born ten years ago. In a field that changes constantly, Peggy feels that she must continue to work at least part-time in order to keep her skills current.

Yet she is subjected to subtle criticism by friends who tell her that she really ought to be at home with her kids. At work she is pulled in the other direction. Although she really prefers part-time work, her supervisor often "needs" her to work extra hours. Periodically she ends up working more than forty hours a week. When she insists on cutting back her hours, she faces her boss' disapproval. "I can't seem to win," she says. "No matter what I do, someone disapproves."

Peggy too is the mother in the middle.

Women Have Always Worked

We hear all the time that "more women are working outside the home," and a quick look at official data on labor force participation shows that this is true. But lost in all the rhetoric about women working is a focus on the change among mothers: the most dramatic change in women's labor force participation has been the increase among married women with children. A change from 28 percent of mothers in the labor force in 1960 to 69 percent in 1994[1]—an increase of two and a half times—is a seismic shift that has altered the landscape of American motherhood.

But lost also is a recognition of the revolution we've experienced as American mothers in the way we work—and where we work.

Women have always worked. Let's be clear about that. We have an amazing legacy of strong, hardworking women as our heritage:

- from the Pilgrim women of Plymouth Rock who braved the tempests of the Atlantic Ocean to help settle the New World
- to the Daughters of Liberty, who refused to drink English tea and spun cloth and made shirts for the soldiers of the Continental Army in the Revolutionary War, helping to establish our nation on the principles of the natural rights of man—even though it would be more than a century before those fundamental rights were extended to them
- to the Lowell mill girls, who worked thirteen hours a day in factories whose windows were nailed shut to preserve moisture for the cloth
- to the black slave women who strapped their children to their backs and kept picking cotton
- to the pioneer women who trudged alongside the Conestoga wagons over the Great Plains, helping expand the boundaries of our great nation
- to Rosie the Riveter, who helped us win a world war
- to the countless women in every generation whose selfless volunteer work in churches, schools, and communities has always formed the backbone of numerous national social reform movements (from abolition to suffrage to temperance and civil rights) and provided the muscle required by thousands of local community service organizations (from United Way drives to PTAs

to Meals on Wheels to Salvation Army shelters to Mothers Against Drunk Driving).

In every century, in every time, heroic women have worked hard, bettered themselves, their families, and their communities, and changed the face of our nation.

But never before in our history have so many mothers of young children gone off to work away from home in the marketplace while entrusting their children to someone else's care. Never before in our history have women caring full-time for their children in their homes been so isolated and so devalued.

What we are seeing today is not so much an increase in women working as the entrenchment of the modern separation of work from home, family, and community.

The Unnoticed Revolution

While it is true that more mothers are working outside the home than ever before, the real, unreported story is which mothers are working. As it turns out, the group of mothers with the biggest increase in labor force participation are those with children under six years of age—precisely the ones with the greatest child care responsibilities. In the past three decades, the percentage of these mothers in the workforce has tripled, going from 20 percent in 1960 to 62 percent in 1994.

It is this increase—women's work choices that affect the youngest children—that is particularly troubling: of all children under the age of six, 56 percent have mothers in the labor force. This is up from only 29 percent in 1970.

The mothers of babies under three years of age increased their workforce participation from approximately one in three in 1975 to nearly three out of five in 1994. And 66 percent of those work full-time. Most surprising of all, though, are the mothers of babies: according to the most recent data (1994), more than half (54 percent) of all babies one year old and younger have mothers in the workforce. This is up from 31 percent in 1975.[2]

These are the statistics. But what do they really mean?

Sociologist Amitai Etzioni puts this changing trend into perspective when he writes:

> Consider for a moment parenting as an industry. As farming declined, most fathers left to work away from home generations ago. Over the past twenty years, millions of American mothers have sharply curtailed their work in the "parenting industry" by moving to work outside the home. . . . At the same time, a much smaller number of child care personnel moved into the parenting industry. If this were any other business, say, shoemaking, and more than half of the labor force had been lost and replaced with fewer, less-qualified hands and still we asked the shoemakers to produce the same number of shoes of the same quality, we would be considered crazy. But this is what happened to parenting.[3]

The cold statistics only bespeak the trend in the "parenting industry" we call motherhood. It's the heartfelt human voices that remind us that behind the statistics are real mothers and their babies. Behind the statistics is Peggy. And Kathy. And Liz. And Allison. And Ellen. And Maria. And Victoria. And all the rest of us who know how it feels to be a mother in the middle.

PART I:

Mothers in the Middle

One

No-Woman's-Land

Motherhood is the gift of God to women.

Mother Teresa
1995 United Nations World Conference
on the Rights of Women

Sarah cradled her three-month-old son, Simon, in the crook of her elbow and tried to get him to take the bottle of formula. He resisted with full baby-protest: arched back, flailing legs, and pitiful cry.

"I just don't know what to do," said Sarah in a mixture of pain, bewilderment, and embarrassment. "The doctor says he's probably OK, but Simon's been constipated for over a week, and he seems to be so uncomfortable."

The small group of mothers gathered for a stroller outing nodded sympathetically but felt helpless to offer much other than the usual suggestions—the cradle carry and tummy rub, both of which Sarah had already tried with little success. It was obvious to everyone, including Sarah, that what Simon really wanted—and needed—was to return to nursing. Formula clearly didn't agree with his newborn digestive system.

Finally the cry became a whimper, and Simon gave up and took the bottle. Since it was a beautiful fall day, the group strolled toward the river. Sarah, still noticeably troubled by her baby's distress, explained that he had to learn to take the bottle so that she could return to work.

"I cry all the time," she said, "but this really seems to be the best decision for us."

The decision was especially hard because Sarah and her husband had wanted a baby for a long time. Simon was conceived after expensive infertility treatments. Then when Sarah became pregnant, her husband took a job in another city, partly because the move offered a cheaper cost of living. It was also a promotion for her husband professionally. The new position was definitely a step up the ladder for him, and even though the job was not immediately lucrative, the career move could mean a long-term payoff. Unfortunately, they hadn't anticipated losing money—so much money—on the sale of their house.

"You know the hardest thing, though?" Sarah asked. "I called some friends of mine from home to talk about how tough this is for me—particularly since I thought I wouldn't have to work if we moved. And my friends immediately said, 'Oh, you're making the wrong decision. You should be home with your baby.'"

Sarah is the mother in the middle. She's caught in the cross fire of the mommy wars. Stuck out there in No-Woman's-Land, she feels torn between two warring factions: career women on one side, faced off against at-home moms on the other. She feels judged and rejected by both. She feels mothers at home are silently criticizing her priorities, but she doesn't feel part of the "sisterhood" of career women either. At this point in her life, she doesn't want to pound on that glass ceiling; she really just wants to be with her baby.

Ambushed by Love

Detroit News reporter Marney Rich Keenan wrote this about the birth of her daughter:

> On January 29, at 1:08 p.m., she came quickly—like a fish darting downstream—and in that split second before birth, her father's words—"We got our lit-

tle girl"—redefined who I was and what I expected
of myself.

Life is slower, quieter. I sit on the couch and
watch as my daughter absorbs the spring breeze quiv-
ering in the lace curtains behind me. She is enthralled
with the wind, and I with her. Sometimes the wonder is so powerful, I find it hard to believe she is
mine. And yet I cannot imagine what life was like
without her.

What used to take precedence in my life—work,
friends, all the worries and concerns that used to con-
sume me—have all moved down the ladder of priorities. Everything else can wait—her needs come
before all others.

When she went back to work, Marney felt that she was
abandoning her daughter:

It seemed to me that I was being asked to deny
my own maternal instincts. To forgo nurturing my
infant because that is evidently outdated in the liberated world in which we live.

"You'll get used to it," my career-minded friends
said. I didn't want to get used to it, over it, or above it.
I didn't want to miss her less. . . . I want to be there
when she discovers ants make hills, roses have thorns,
and the moon is so big it follows you at night.[1]

Marney is also the mother in the middle. For her, like so
many of the mothers we talked to, the mommy wars are
merely a reflection of the internal battle she wages within herself. She feels torn between her heart and her soul. Having a
baby was a stunning experience for her; she had no idea how
much this little being would tug at her heart. She was clearly
caught by surprise when she suddenly found herself reevalu-
ating her entire life, in light of this new life that had been given
to her care.

For while her heart called out for her to stay and be with her baby, being a professional was obviously an important part of her identity and her soul.

So she too is caught in no-woman's-land.

The Search for Answers

What did we say to Sarah when she told us her story? To the other women who talked to us?

As women and mothers who know from personal experience what it feels like to be the mother in the middle, we are reluctant to give quick-and-easy, prescriptive advice to our friends. We don't believe there is only one True Path to Ultimate Motherhood. What works for one family doesn't necessarily work for another. What is good stewardship of gifts and resources for one woman could be wrong for her sister or her friend. This is a book about choices—choices that include, allow for, and encourage motherhood.

It would be nice, actually, if there *were* just one way—if the simplistic question "Are you going back to work?" reflected reality. But it doesn't. It's not that easy.

Because our choices always have consequences.

It's the weightiness of those consequences that has turned these most personal of decisions into the Mommy Wars. It does matter—it matters a lot—what choices we make about balancing work and caring for our children. And we want those choices validated by others. Most of all, deep down we really do wish it were easy. Straightforward. Uncomplicated. Cut and dried. We want to have a role to slip into. Guideposts. A pattern to follow. Unfortunately, over the last few decades, the mother in the middle has felt trapped by a feminine role model too often shrouded in . . .

Myths and Mirages

Yearning for simplicity and uniformity, we have constructed "boxes" to fit mothers into. Our unique individuality as women and mothers makes for loose ends, but never mind—we just tie them up in tight little balls, stuff them back into the boxes, and slam the tops down. Craving easy answers, people become polarized. The debate has become a war: the mommy war.

On one side is the superwoman. You know her: she can "bring home the bacon, fry it up in a pan ..." Basically, she does it all. She's on the fast track, blazing new paths for women in the workplace—and all the while, she's a perfect mom, baking cookies and making Halloween costumes. Let's face it: we may hate her, but she's the myth most women feel pressure to emulate—she's the new-woman icon immortalized forever by Madison Avenue.

On the other side is the stay-at-home mom. She's the woman in the pageboy, chauffeuring her kids around in the Dodge minivan. Let's face it: she's a sweet person, but you really wouldn't want to talk to her at a dinner party. What does she do all day, anyway? We know the bonbons and soap operas are a cliché, but—well, who does watch those soaps?

It's the Superwoman Myth vs. the Stay-at-Home Mirage. Both are cartoon soldiers. Neither really exists. Caught between these conflicting caricatures is the real-life mother in the middle.

Superwoman is a myth because no human being can be that perfect—and do that much. A whole generation of women have exhausted themselves trying to do it all: in her landmark study of women and work, *The Second Shift*, sociologist Arlie Hochschild found that women, in trying to meet superwoman demands, work an extra month of twenty-four-hour days a year. *An extra month!* Hochschild reported that many of the women she talked to "talked about sleep the way a hungry person talks about food."[2]

By contrast, many people have a shimmery image of the stay-at-home mom's life as one of ease, routine, and intellectual waste. But behind that chimerical vision of an oasis filled with yuppie homegrown herb gardens is likely to be a young mom who feels abandoned in a desert. She used to have an independent identity; now she's submerged in diapers, struggling to cope all alone in a suburban neighborhood that becomes a ghost town between the hours of eight and six. By the time she glances out the window to see her neighbors streaming home again—at which point she might have some adult interaction—she's caught up in the whirl of baths and jammies, looking forward to a night of interrupted sleep. She's exhausted too.

Many real at-home mothers with older children laugh at the very term "stay-at-home mom." For they find themselves so seldom at home.

One mother, interviewed for Deborah's book *Motherhood Stress*, told her:

> Some weeks I feel more a chauffeur or a taxi driver than a mother. I drop kids off at three different schools every morning ... which means three different stops every afternoon, too. That doesn't include scout meetings, ball games, piano lessons, children's choir practice at church, or kids' visits to friends' homes.[3]

The time many at-home mothers spend in their cars feels just as isolated—and just as stressful—as being at home with small children.

Living the day-to-day grind between the myth and the mirage is the mother in the middle.

We see her and hear her voice everywhere we turn. A recent newspaper advice column offered this exchange:

Dear Abby:

> I feel compelled to write to the stay-at-home mom who felt overworked, underappreciated, and suffocated. I know how she feels. I have four small children under five years old, and I haven't had a "day

off" since the first one was born. Many people think I'm lucky, because I don't "have to work." Staying home with children *is* work. My husband looks forward to the weekends, when he doesn't have to work, and just when I think I'll have him around to help, he decides to go golfing, because he needs to relax after working all week. My sisters have commented that I used to be fun and funny. It's hard to be quick witted when you're up all night with a new baby, then up again at dawn with the other kids. As a single-income family, we can't afford to hire help or baby-sitters. But your column helped me. After I wrote you this letter, I showed it (and the letter in your column) to my husband. He agreed I needed a "sanity day," and he's planning to stay home with the kids one day next week. I'm going to dress up and go to lunch with my sisters. Thanks, Abby, for my first day off!

Stressed at Home in Pa.

Dear Abby:

I just read the letter from "Not OK Kaye," the stay-at-home mom who said her only relief from full-time motherhood is her part-time job. My problem is exactly the opposite. I *have* to work outside the home. I wish I could be home more often with my two young children. I feel as if they are being raised by day care. I hate dragging them out of the house when it's barely light, and not seeing them until it is dark again. My house goes unattended all week, so my weekends are spent doing laundry, vacuuming, and running errands—a week's worth of housework in two days. I'd do anything to be home more and watch my children play and grow. I wish I were in Kaye's shoes. . . .

Homemaker Wanna-Be[4]

The mother in the middle is struggling. We understand that. As we talked with other mothers all across this nation, we heard many voices. We heard voices of longing: "I wish I didn't have to work," one mother suddenly volunteered to us in a conversation that had nothing to do with our research and nothing to do with mothering. We heard loneliness: "I miss my job and adult conversation." We heard voices of regret: "I squandered the years when my babies were young," said a forty-year-old mother, the president of her company. From others, we heard voices of fatigue, yearning, and defensiveness.

But even in the midst of these voices, we also heard voices of joy and satisfaction. And from them all, we heard voices of mothers who dearly love their babies.

Can't Buy Me Love

That mother love is a first principle. Babies need that love. Renowned psychologist Urie Bronfenbrenner has explained that what children need in order to develop properly is to have "a strong, mutual, irrational, emotional attachment [with someone] who is committed to the child's well-being and development, preferably for life."

Irrational? In other words, someone needs to be "crazy about the kid!" Bronfenbrenner points out that each child needs to feel that there is an adult who believes they are uniquely special "even though objectively the adult may well know that this is not the case." Isn't that precisely the definition of mother love? Bronfenbrenner calls this "the illusion that comes with love."[5]

Can you buy an illusion?

With modernity and mechanization—and with more women entering the workforce—we've begun to pay others for most of the services that our great-grandmothers used to perform in the home. We eat out (1994 was the first year that more meals were prepared outside of the home than inside the home); we take shirts to the dry cleaner's; we purchase bread at the grocery; and we select all of our clothing from stores or catalogs. Ironically, some of our mothers' low-status jobs have even gained great élan now that they've been transferred to the marketplace. We pay exorbitant prices for great chefs; pricey interior designers instruct us in the appropriate colors of wallpaper and paint; and clothing designers have become worldwide celebrities.

Somehow along the way, ever so subtly, the idea crept in that motherhood could be lumped in as one of those services that could be contracted out.

Can you buy an illusion?

Virtual Reality?

Part of the problem is that today home, work, and child rearing are separate, isolated endeavors, in a way they never were before. Prior to industrialization, children grew up in the midst of an adult world, with work happening all around them. As essential contributors to the day-to-day work and survival of the household, women were valued. Mothers and their children were not segregated off in their own shadowy world, separate and unequal, existing as mere reflections of the "real" work going on in the "real" world.

––––––––––––––––

The scene: a party celebrating a recent wedding, to which many coworkers of the couple had been invited. Children were welcome, so one man brought his wife and three children. As they entered, the bride rushed over enthusiastically.

"Chuck!" she exclaimed. "It's so fun to see you out of context!"

Without a pause and with the slightest of smiles on his face, he gently responded, "But Charmaine, this"—he gestured to his wife and children—"is my context."

Where are we in context? We've lost sight of how valuable being a mother is. Actually, we've lost sight of how valuable being a parent is. For most people, men and women, the context that makes the most sense these days is in the workplace, not the home. That's how we all define ourselves.

The question always seems to be, "What do you do?"

Margaret used to be the Midwest editor of one of the premier trade journals in her field. Motherhood was one of those things she assumed she'd get to eventually, so she didn't give it that much thought—until she couldn't get pregnant. Suddenly she realized what a priority being a mother was for her.

So it was with great rejoicing that Heather finally arrived on the scene when Margaret was in her early thirties. Margaret never even considered staying at her job and threw herself into motherhood with relish and joy. It was an adjustment, certainly, but she was committed to making it work and being as successful in this new venture as she had been professionally.

"I really don't miss my job," she said. "In fact, the editing and writing projects that I'm doing on the side take me away from Heather more than I want. I wouldn't do them," she explained, "but my husband really wants me to keep working.

"Actually, he'd have already persuaded me to be back working full-time if I didn't feel so strongly about staying home with Heather," she admitted a little sheepishly. "Ron feels as if he's supporting me in my little hobby."

Is it any wonder so many mothers are choosing to enter the workforce full-time?

Moving toward the Middle

Isn't there some other middle we could carve out for Sarah, Margaret, and ourselves? Does it have to be a choice between our children and our work? Why does improving women's opportunities in society involve leaving our babies behind? Why should defending women's rights involve devaluing motherhood?

Many women today are coming to realize that they wish they could spend—or wish they had spent—more time raising their children.

Part of the devaluing of motherhood is the perception that being a mother is a sacrifice of either career or economic income.

It is. And more.

It's very tempting to whitewash and sentimentalize the decision to make motherhood a priority. It would be easier if we could be glib about the costs of putting careers on hold and giving up a second income. But the truth is that for many women, if not most, the choice is costly. Any discussion of moving toward the middle must recognize that fact.

During the 1995 United Nations World Conference on the Rights of Women, motherhood became a very controversial issue, so Mother Teresa sent this message to the assembled delegates in Beijing:

> Motherhood is the gift of God to women. . . . Yet
> we can destroy this gift of motherhood, especially by
> the evil of abortion, but also by thinking that other
> things—like jobs or positions—are more important
> than loving, than giving oneself to others. . . .[6]

Poets and saints have long tried to teach us that the best gifts in life have a price. And motherhood is one of the highest gifts we can ever be given. Being a good mother has always required sacrifice. And today we often think of that "sacrifice" in terms of career or income. But for so many of the employed women we talked to, the difficult choice is leaving their kids in order to work and abdicating some of their daily role in raising their children. For them, that is the real sacrifice.

Feminine Power

Is "sacrifice" in today's terminology just a hidden code word for "Ozzie and Harriet"? Are we constructing our own box labeled "True Motherhood," with a June Cleaver picture glued on the front?

This accusation is a central volley in the mommy wars: if the discussion turns to full-time motherhood, the stay-at-home-mom mirage is trotted out. In this quintessential version, the mirage takes the form of Donna Reed in high heels and pearls, vacuuming her spotless living room while a stew simmers on the stove. It's all part of the polarization of the mommy wars: you're either cast as a with-it woman of the nineties who "works"—a superwoman—or you're a cartoon throwback to the fifties.

So what's the mother in the middle to do? We're not talking about going back to the fifties. Far from providing the perfect model of true motherhood, the fifties were a part of the problem. A society organized so that mothers and children are isolated in the suburbs and so that economically productive work is separated from the home is the dilemma—not the solution.

We want to move forward: searching for peace in the mommy wars is an attainable goal. However, peace must come on two levels. First, we must dispel the myths and mirages and rediscover a substantive role for women in our society today. But we also need to find a personal peace for the mother in the middle. We believe no-woman's-land could become middle ground. Not a mushy middle born of an uneasy truce. Rather, a middle born of what Aristotle called the golden mean: true balance. A balance between heart and soul, an integration of our responsibility to sacrifice and serve as mothers and our need to cultivate the personal gifts that form our core identity.

We believe the middle is high ground—we will have to climb up from either side and find common ground at the top. From there we can pull our children up and out of the shadows.

That would be real feminine power.

Abigail Adams wrote a letter to her husband John Adams while he was at the Continental Congress in 1776, gently reminding him of the innate power women hold:

But you must remember that arbitrary power is like most other things which are very hard, very liable to be broken; and, notwithstanding all your wise laws and maxims, we have it in our power, not only to free ourselves, but to subdue our masters, and, without violence, throw both your natural and legal authority at our feet.[7]

The tragedy of the mommy wars is that it misdirects and dissipates the power that is ours. We have it in our power! We need not crusade for power; we have it. But we haven't used properly our intrinsic feminine power. We have used our power in this century to better the position of women, but have we left our children behind? Maybe it's time we rethink motherhood again for the twenty-first century.

———————————

As Laura stepped out into the sunshine and looked across the playground filled with children, she spotted her one-and-a-half-year-old daughter, Ruth, sitting motionless in the middle swing of a three-seat swing set. Laura's aerobics class met in the basement of a church that also housed a day care center. Today the four children from the aerobics class were playing on the playground outside, with their baby-sitter and the thirty or more kids from the day care.

Laura thought Ruth looked a little lost and bewildered in the midst of the bustling playground. Quickly Laura closed the distance between them.

"Look at you, Ruthie!" Laura cried out. "You're swinging! What fun!"

Ruth's head jerked around and she broke into a huge grin, squirming with delight as her mother approached. Laughing together with Ruth and pushing her swing, Laura hadn't paid any attention to the two little girls sitting in the swings on either side of her daughter.

"Look at me," cried the little brunette to the left. As she began wriggling in her seat, frantically swinging her legs to move the swing, the blond to the right called out too.

"Look at me!" she cried.

Suddenly Laura's attention was riveted on these other two eager little ones. Since there were only two other adults to supervise all of the children on the playground, they too had been sitting motionless on the swings, with no one to push them. Almost frantically they competed with each other and Ruth to hold Laura's attention.

Look at me! Look at me!

This cry for attention is echoing all across our nation as more and more children spend more and more of their time in child care.

While we've revolutionized the world for ourselves, striding into the full sun, we've left our children in the shadows. They take steps that no one notices; they sit on swings that no one pushes. They too are stuck in no-woman's-land.

Look at me!

Yes, we have it in our power—but have we really freed ourselves?

Two

The Feminine Mystake

*The care of children in their infancy is one of the grand
duties annexed to the female character by nature.*

Mary Wollstonecraft
A Vindication of the Rights of Woman, 1792[1]

It was standing room only. The former prime minister of Ireland sat near the front while latecomers, unable to find space to squeeze in and join the hundreds inside, stood quietly outside. The cars carrying mourners to the service had stretched out over a mile from the house to the church. They had all come to honor the life of one tiny Irish woman, Rosaleen Kenny.

Rosaleen herself would have been astonished. She wasn't famous. She married at seventeen and always lived on a farm. Her eulogy didn't include homilies to a long list of accomplishments—no, her achievements were sitting in the pews: all ten of her surviving children and twenty-six of her grandchildren, who had flown in from all around the world.

Rosaleen Kenny had never had a career, so she had eagerly asked about the work her granddaughter Michelle was doing. She had been so impressed! Her granddaughter, she had thought, was awfully important. But in the end, it was Rosaleen's life that left Michelle wondering what, ultimately, was truly important.

"I think about the contribution she made to the world through her children and her grandchildren," said Michelle, "and I can't imagine not leaving something like that behind."

Michelle is young, single, and avidly pursuing her career, but the dramatic contrast between her life and her grandmother's made her stop and reevaluate her own priorities. "My grandmother's death drastically changed my perspective," she said. "Before, I would very easily get upset about work if I didn't get something that I wanted. When I didn't move as fast up the career ladder as I wanted to, I felt that it was really hurting my career. I felt it indicated that I was a failure. After her death it really hit home to me that work is not the most important thing in life for me."

They turned out by the hundreds to honor a woman who was ... a mother. Just a mother.

Now, born only two generations later, Michelle isn't alone in getting the subtle message that being a mother isn't an honor anymore. Many women have found that being introduced as a "mother" at parties is a guaranteed conversation-stopper.

Mary Kay Berger, a former marketing executive turned at-home mom, was featured in a *Ladies Home Journal* profile. Berger, who used to pull down seventy thousand dollars a year in business, found that the way people responded to her now that she was a mother had suddenly changed.

> At social functions when people ask, "What do you do?" I say, "I stay home and take care of my girls," and that pretty much ends the conversation. I sometimes want to say, "Well, let me tell you about what I *used* to do. I used to be one of *you*."[2]

This is a common story among moms today: nearly every one has a story of an awkward social silence after fessing up to being *just* a mom. Outside the closed society of other at-home mothers, the world seems to have lost its ability to relate to motherhood. As a result, even mothers who are otherwise confident and at ease in their parenting decisions acknowledge a tendency to de-emphasize their role as a mother when meeting new people.

Melanie says she is one of the lucky ones who has it all: she stays home with her young son but still manages to write a successful newspaper column and appear regularly on television as a political commentator. She doesn't make a lot of money, but it's the optimal situation for her. She feels sorry, she says, for her "sisters" who don't have the same opportunity to feel so fulfilled. Press her and she feels no conflict over her choice to stay at home and looks forward to having a lot more children.

Nevertheless, she admits to hedging occasionally on introductions.

"Sometimes I'll just say I have an eighteen-month-old and he keeps me busy and that's kind of my job right now," she explains, "or I'll just say I write a newspaper column and do some television commentary. And it really does depend—I can think of a couple situations where when people have asked, 'What are you doing now?' I definitely will play up the professional side, and I catch myself doing that. So obviously there's a little ambivalence there."

Sherry is the mother of two vivacious little girls, Carrie and Maggie, who arrived in quick succession after Sherry finished her graduate work in kinesiology. She teaches on the college level one day a week, just to keep her hand in the game. She doesn't want to give up her career, because she invested herself in her graduate degree. And—bottom line—she just loves working with college students.

Still, despite the fact that she and her husband endure occasional financial struggles, she remains highly committed to being an at-home mom for her children, because her mother was always home for her. She considers herself fortunate to have a lot of friends who have made the same choices she has. Virtually everyone she knows, she says, stays home with their children and works part-time.

So the only real stress Sherry feels over her decisions about work and parenting is internal: maintaining the balancing act between enough time at home and enough time at school.

Nevertheless, like Melanie, she feels an inner impulse to emphasize her professional self over motherhood—even with other mothers. "When people ask me what I do, I say, 'I'm mostly a mom, but I do this . . . ,'" she said a little sheepishly. "So I know that's my cop-out. I don't ever just say, 'I'm a mom.'"

But it's not just at-home moms who feel their role as mothers is something they can't talk about. Employed mothers can feel it, too. *McCall's* magazine ran an article called "The Six Mistakes Working Mothers Make," which included a caution against appearing . . . too motherly. "At work, too many reminders of your children—photos, drawings—can send the message that your mind is more on home than on your job."

Their advice?

"Limit yourself to one cherished photo of each child, and perhaps one or two pieces of your children's artwork."[3] Could we ever imagine similar advice being given to fathers in the pages of *Forbes* or *Fortune*?

The bias is subtle. After all, this is America—"motherhood and apple pie." But the devaluing message comes through loud and clear in the different emphasis given the two sides of the work-family dilemma: while the rhetoric is about "balancing" work and career with motherhood, the coverage is heavily tilted toward work. A typical article will explore how to ensure that being a mom doesn't interfere with—or derail—one's career. Where are the corresponding articles on ensuring that one's career doesn't interfere with being a mom?

A typical example is the special report "Mothers at Work" run by *Cosmopolitan*, with a lead article entitled "Can You Be *Somebody* and a Mommy Too?" Well, the answer was a resounding yes: "You can have babies and a big-league career," affirmed the author.[4]

But let's back up for a minute. Isn't there a clear implication that being a "mommy" isn't enough to qualify as a "somebody"?

Not all women become mothers, of course. But for those who do, it is a central, defining experience of their lives. Being a parent, for men *and* women, is a sacred duty; it is a high and awesome responsibility, unlike any other we are given in life. Nevertheless, in our society today, becoming a mother, while celebrated on a rhetorical level, is devalued on another, more fundamental level.

A Woman's Place?

How did we get to the place where motherhood has become so empty of social content and viewed so paternalistically? Let's take a quick glance back at the history of women and work.

A woman's place has always been in the home, right?

Actually, this stereotype is a relatively recent occurrence. For thousands of years, the people of our world lived as hunters and gatherers. Typically, men tended to be the hunters and women tended to be gatherers, although historical evidence indicates that in many such societies, women did some hunting and men did some gathering. Women were working, contributing members of the tribe most of their lives. A mother's work was such that she could easily stop to breast-feed a baby or care for her young children.

The shift of society from hunting and gathering to agriculture changed life dramatically. But on the farm, men still took those roles that required longer absences from the house.

And women assumed those jobs that were near the house and could be interrupted to feed and care for children.

In both types of societies, for thousands of years, women took on that work that could be easily interwoven with the care of children. Men and women were mutually interdependent. Children were considered valuable, since each child would grow up to be another member of the tribe or another pair of hands on the farm. As children were valued, so motherhood and its tasks were valued.

We certainly do not mean to say that in either of these types of cultures, life was easy. For most of history, life has required hard work from both men and women. The ordinary woman of preindustrial society worked hard—but her work allowed for the care of her children. She was not asked to choose between productive work and her children's needs.

And we're not saying that women had complete equality with men. Throughout human history and across most cultures, men tended to acquire political power while enjoying legal rights and educational opportunities that were often and unjustly denied to women. (Although it seems only fair to note that until recent generations, it was a relatively small minority of the elite men in most cultures who exercised significant political power or obtained formal educations.)

Gabrielle Palmer tells us, in her book *The Politics of Breastfeeding:*

> When people refer to the woman's place in the home, they forget that before the Industrial Revolution, everyone's place was in the home. The household was the production unit and every enterprise was inextricably bound up with the family. . . . The majority of women were workers who participated fully in economic life in a way that was taken for granted. . . . Though this society was patriarchal in the sense that men had the authority, women were active partici-

pants in economic life and the division of labour was not rigid. The historian Peter Laslett quotes an eighteenth-century observer of rural life who said, "In the long winter evenings, the husband cobbles shoes, mends the family clothes, and attends to the children while the wife spins."[5]

Ruth Schwartz Cowan, researching the history of housework for her book *More Work For Mother*, read dozens of diaries and hundreds of letters written by people who lived in this country between 1660 and 1860. She writes:

> Although housework was socially defined as "woman's work," in reality the daily exigencies of agrarian life meant that men and women had to work in tandem in order to undertake any single life-sustaining chore. The relations between the sexes were reciprocal: women assisted men in the fields and men assisted women in the house.[6]

When production moved from the home into the factory during the Industrial Revolution, life changed dramatically again. Machines took over more and more of the labor to produce things that had traditionally been made at home. Households no longer produced cloth—they bought it. Families ceased to make candles and instead purchased kerosene. Instead of chopping wood, people bought coal.

As men left the home for the factory or the office, where they could readily make enough money to more than pay for what had been produced at home, and as children left the home for compulsory school attendance, women stayed home, alone. Ms. Cowan observes:

> The household continued to be the locale in which meals, clean laundry, healthy children, and well-fed adults were "produced." ... Modern technology enabled the American housewife of 1950 to produce single-handedly what her counterpart of 1850 needed

a staff of three or four to produce: a middle-class standard of health and cleanliness for herself, her spouse,
and her children. . . . The time that housewives had
once spent in preserving strawberries and stitching
petticoats was being spent in driving to stores, shopping, and waiting in lines, and the energy that had
once gone into bedside care of the sick was diverted
into driving a feverish child to the doctor or racing to
the railroad station to pick up a relative or taking the
baseball team to the next town for a game. The automobile had become to the American housewife . . . the
vehicle through which she did much of her significant
work and the work locale where she could most often
be found.[7]

Claudia Golden, an award-winning Harvard economist
who wrote a book on women's labor history, established new
data on women's work that shows much higher labor force
participation for married women in the nineteenth century by
including what she calls the "hidden market work" of married
women. "Hidden work" is her term for two factors: unpaid
home labor and home production of goods.

As industrialization took hold of the American market,
married women were slowly stripped of their place in the
economy. Golden explains:

Changes in the marketplace would have wide-
ranging repercussions on the social context of household work. Daughters were to spend less time in the
household performing chores alongside their mothers
and under their tutelage. Wives and mothers were to
become increasingly isolated during the workday.
From 1850 to 1950, the working time of married
women within the household was separated first from
their spouses and other workers, next and most ironically from their own children, and finally from other
married women who had entered the workforce.

Their value, as producers of market goods and as instructors in household skill, would become steadily diminished over that century.[8]

The woman of the 1950s and 1960s still spent many hours doing housework. But unlike preindustrial mothers, she found herself isolated in her home, without the help and company of husband, children, or household helpers.

Industry had freed her from many tasks once assigned to women. But most of the jobs women had been relieved of were the ones that produced a tangible, satisfying end result: candle making, quilting, the designing and sewing of clothes for the family, and the canning and preserving of food.

The work left for the housewives of the fifties and sixties tended to be the supervision of machines—vacuum cleaners, mixers, washing machines, ovens, and so on. Work that was repetitious drudgery: sweeping and mopping; folding and ironing clothes; scrubbing bathrooms. And work that was stressful: driving children to and from activities; waiting in line; doing the family shopping.

The one meaningful job that no machine was able to duplicate was the nurturing of children. But this work was made more difficult by the isolation from other mothers and support systems and by the cultural presence of "experts" who constantly gave volumes of conflicting advice to mothers.

By the 1950s and 1960s, this division of labor between men and women had become solidified. But it also disturbed what had been the traditional balance of personal power between husbands and wives. Instead of sharing in the responsibility for the direct provision of the family's daily needs, many women became entirely dependent on their husband's income for their basic provision. In families where the husband loved, and was committed to, his wife, this presented little problem. But in many families, the husband began to consider his paycheck to be "his money" and failed to fairly value his wife's contribution.

In a preindustrial society, a husband, however selfish or unloving he might have been, could hardly have kept his wife from eating produce from their garden, eggs from their chickens, or any food she helped gather. But in modern society, the income a husband earns can be hidden or disguised, making a woman in our culture much more vulnerable to the goodwill of her partner than women a hundred or a thousand years ago.

Certainly, many mothers in postindustrial society were secure in their marriages. And many housewives of the mid–twentieth century found satisfaction and fulfillment through charity work, involvement with their church, the daily enjoyment of children, or the pursuit of education.

But other mothers of the 1950s and 1960s found themselves with little work that seemed meaningful or well respected. They looked around at friends whose husbands were seeking divorce, and they felt financially insecure. Is it any wonder, then, that so many women came to feel shuffled to the fringes of contemporary society, unfulfilled by the work left for them to do, worried by their unprecedented economic vulnerability, and frustrated by a drastic shift in the traditional balance of personal power between men and women?

The stage was set for . . .

The Feminine Mystake

In 1963 Betty Friedan, the founder of the National Organization for Women (NOW), published *The Feminine Mystique*, a book many credit with launching a "revolution" and igniting the modern feminist movement. American women, Friedan said, were suffering from a problem—"the problem that has no name." In defining this problem, Friedan described suburban housewives living lives of quiet desperation, trapped in homes characterized as "comfortable concentration camps," and devoid of purposeful work, leaving them "afraid to ask even of herself the silent question—'Is this all?'"

As Friedan spelled out her description of the problem, she concluded that:

> It is far more important than anyone recognizes.... It may well be the key to our future as a nation and a culture. We can no longer ignore that voice within women that says: "I want something more than my husband and my children and my home."[9]

But is that voice just within women? Both men and women need "something more"—something that helps them define who they are, that something that gets them out of bed in the morning and makes them feel alive. This is part of the human condition. Her description of the symptoms was correct: many women were suffering from an emptiness in their souls; others were lost and rudderless, without a sense of purpose in their lives.

Friedan's essential conclusion was that society's narrow, constricting, idealized view of womanhood, which she termed the "feminine mystique," had stifled women by defining for them only one role in society—occupation: housewife-mother. She described capable, talented, well-educated women whose vision for their lives was limited to "soapy dishpans," and who were living vicariously through their children and becoming increasingly dependent on their husbands and sex for any spark of excitement or thrill in their lives.

Her criticism of this limited and limiting vision of femininity, to the extent that it was an accurate portrayal of women's lives, was valid. It is not healthy for women to totally submerge their identities in the lives of their husbands and children. It is not good for marriages when women have no independent interests and have no challenges outside their intimate relationships. Every woman has talents and abilities that she has a responsibility to cultivate.

Being a vibrant human being, for women *and* men, requires developing a strong sense of identity. But according to Friedan, it was this feminine mystique that prevented women from finding their identities. The mystique, complained Friedan, had mis-led women into thinking "the highest value and the only com-mitment for women is the fulfillment of their own femininity." And, she argued, it had stifled women by convincing them "the root of women's troubles in the past is that women envied men, women tried to be like men, instead of accepting their own nature, which can find fulfillment only in sexual passivity, male domination, and nurturing maternal love."[10]

Consider for a moment the message of that last quote.

Is nurturing maternal love really in the same category as sexual passivity and male domination? Friedan would never say so outright—indeed, she writes eloquently about her own mothering and grandmothering experiences—but the clear implication here is that mother love is only for insipid women who are hung up sexually and are dominated by men.

Friedan spotted a number of serious symptoms and clearly struck a responsive chord—many women were struggling with a problem as old as time itself: developing an inner sense of self. But her diagnosis was wrong—motherhood was not the significant cause of the problem.

This misdiagnosis is the heart of the problem facing the mother in the middle today. In the struggle to gain women their legitimate place in society, motherhood has been dis-torted and miscast as one of the primary societal institutions repressing women. And that was feminism's first mystake.

Friedan's famous "problem without a name" was in fact an identity problem. But naming it didn't solve anything. And misdiagnosing the cause only compounded the problem when it led to Friedan dispensing a wrong and potentially dangerous prescription. She convinced many women they could and would find a higher, truer, more liberated identity if they turned away from home and family-related roles to devote their lives to more meaningful, challenging, and satisfying "careers." And that, as we will see in the next chapter and throughout this book, was the second mystake.

If anything, with the onset of the mommy wars, the feminine identity crisis has only worsened. And not just with mothers reluctant to introduce themselves as such. Whenever and wherever we talked with women about motherhood and their role in society, the omnipresent theme of identity came up again and again.

Who Am I?

Dorinne, the mother of three girls, ages two to seven, had found an identity for herself in the professional world, as a designer. She told us she's had quite a struggle feeling good about herself and her primary identity as a mother today. Dorinne said:

"I tell you, I bought into the whole women's lib thing. I subscribed to *Ms.* I was a card-carrying member of NOW. The whole thing. I bought into all that crap and had my little life shook up real big when I realized a lot of it isn't true. Now, the feminists don't mean you have the choice to stay home; the only choice they see is to go to work. I feel as if the whole feminist movement devalues motherhood, and that's where I got my opinions.

"The first several years were hard, because I had devalued motherhood. I had felt that women who stayed at home with children were too dumb to do anything else. My self-esteem was so low, I ended up in counseling to help me deal with it.

"I had a lot of growing and learning to do. I had believed all that stuff I'd heard as a feminist. For example, that boys and girls are exactly the same, that the only differences are because we've been socialized to think differently, dress differently, and act differently.

"So I bought my first daughter trucks, and they sat and gathered dust while she went and played with her baby dolls. I've had three girls and, dad-blast-it, every one of them has left those trucks just sitting there in the closet.

"There's too much of a difference to say there's no differ-ence between the two. There's a big difference. Celebrating those differences is a growing point. I had a long way to go. I thought I knew all the answers and found out I didn't even know the questions.

"The first year or two, I had just one child and she was real easygoing and mobile. So I went to a few conferences that year. I would meet up with some of my old friends, and they would ask what I was doing now. I would say, 'Well, nothing.'

"That was a hard thing, because my position at work had been a very respected position. When I told people that I was staying home with my daughter, eyebrows shot up. They minded their p's and q's in what they said. But their reaction said it all.

"People who had always respected me and had been quick to seek out my opinion in the past suddenly considered me to be someone who didn't have anything to say. People I had known and interacted with professionally, when they learned I was now at home with my baby daughter, would say, 'Oh, that's nice, sweetie.' Then they would turn around and walk off.

"Part of me felt that way, too. That I no longer had any-thing to say. Now I know that's not true. But at first, I felt as if my life were just diapers and breast-feeding. And those were the only topics of conversation that I could handle. And it really bothered me. It bothered me that I no longer had a title. That I didn't have a 'real' job. I knew I had a brain, but when you tell people you're a mother, they think you don't."

While Dorinne told us she'd finally found real content-ment in an identity that includes motherhood, she admits to still feeling at times as if

"I'm stuck in the middle of a big tug-of-war. I still find the desire to make a name for myself in a career—even if it's an at-home career. I still find a desire to be able to point to some-thing tangible and say, 'I did this.' This year, the only New Year's resolution I made was I want to start designing again.

Part of that is I want to see my name on something again. Part of it is I want to create again. Part of it is I want to see that I've done something concrete. Everything else in my life is not. I feel pulled too, because I want all that and yet I also want to stay home with the kids. So it's back and forth."

Millie is a mother of two who has established a successful part-time desktop publishing business at home. She too talked a lot about identity issues and her conflicted feelings:

"I feel committed to being home for my children as they grow up. At the same time, I know that from the point of view of finding a sense of self-worth, I need work outside of my family. My whole world cannot be successfully reduced to just taking care of my children; that would not make me feel fulfilled, and I feel that—I *know* that—if I did not do anything else, I would be cheating myself.

"But I'm trying to find that solid middle ground. It's just such a fine line that one has to walk. I know that I feel so happy when I'm down in front of that computer and I can get something done—whether it's an article done or an invoice for the card project or creating a new card. It makes me feel that I'm contributing to the world in a bigger picture and a bigger way. Also, the paycheck thing is important. I feel I want to have some money coming in that's mine.

"But it's funny: When I meet other women who are full-time moms, I downplay what I'm doing. And when I meet someone who works full-time, I feel about two inches tall, you know. I feel embarrassed that I'm not working 'as hard as' they are."

Another mom summarized the identity problem mothers face, by observing:

"Society doesn't know where to place moms—are we functional parts of society or just 'part of life'? I hope someday society will realize just how important it is to be a mom—but it looks as if it will take a while."

Yes, an identity crisis among women is still with us. And Betty Friedan wasn't the first or last person to diagnosis motherhood as a major cause.

Running toward the Wrong Goal

During the winter of 1879, many social invitations in Stockholm, Sweden, included a strange postscript: "You are requested not to mention Ibsen's *A Doll's House*." The injunction was needed because of the firestorm that had erupted over Henrik Ibsen's play about a woman's place in society. Ibsen's solution at the conclusion of the play is a fascinating foreshadowing of the feminine mystake.

Ibsen's character, Nora, is a beautiful woman—her husband, Torvald Helmer, calls her his "pretty little songbird." She has few other interests in life besides keeping him happy, taking care of their children, and making their home "cozy." But she does have a secret: many years ago Torvald was desperately ill, and she borrowed the money to save his life. But to do so, she had to forge a signature on the promissory note because, as a wife, she could not legally borrow money on her own without her husband's consent.

The man who lent her the money discovers the forgery, begins blackmailing her, and Torvald finds out about the whole business. Suddenly his "songbird" is a "miserable woman" who should not be allowed to bring up his children.

Torvald's tirade is interrupted by a note from the blackmailer—he has had a change of heart and has sent the IOU back, relieving them of their responsibility. Torvald is overjoyed and tells Nora, "That's the end of that." She is his songbird again.

But Nora has recognized that she is a doll living in a dollhouse. And she decides to leave:

Nora: Tomorrow I shall go home—I mean to
          what was my home. It will be easier for me
          to find some opening there.
Helmer: Oh, in your blind inexperience—
Nora: I must try to gain experience, Torvald.
Helmer: To forsake your home, your husband, and
          your children! And you don't consider what
          the world will say!
Nora: I can pay no heed to that. I only know that
          I must do it.
Helmer: This is monstrous! Can you forsake your
          holiest duties in this way?
Nora: What do you consider my holiest duties?
Helmer: Do I need to tell you that? Your duties to
          your husband and your children.
Nora: I have other duties equally sacred.
Helmer: Impossible! What duties do you mean?
Nora: My duties towards myself.[11]

Like any good lie, this one closely resembles the truth. Of course Nora has duties to herself. Without a doubt, she needs a strong identity to raise her children. But why is it that in fiction, it is so often contrived so that the woman must leave to find herself?

It's the truth vs. a lie: egocentric self-actualization is a counterfeit of self-respect, rooted in responsibilities and accomplishments.

Almost exactly one hundred years later, Nora was back. This time it was the big screen instead of the stage. The story was completely different and modernized, reflecting current issues. But the same persistent theme of feminine identity in need of self-actualization is easily recognized. And it created nearly the same stir: in 1979 *Kramer vs. Kramer* received the Academy Award for best picture.

Joanna Kramer sits at her son's bedside, stroking his hair as he falls asleep. Her fingers trail down his back. "Don't let the bedbugs bite. . . .," she whispers.

Billy responds almost inaudibly, "See you in the morning, Mommy."

She gets up, walks out of the room, and packs her suitcase to leave.

Her husband, Ted, tries to help his son cope with his abandonment as best he can. Finally a letter arrives for Billy, and Ted hurries to give it to him.

"I told you Mom would write before the week was over," says Ted, entering Billy's room. Billy is lying in bed, watching television with the remote control in his hand, covers pulled up to his chin.

"When's she coming back?"

"That's what we're going to find out right now. . . . Let's read it. 'My dearest, sweet Billy . . .' It's for you,"Ted says, looking up.

Billy smiles. Then Ted looks down at the letter and continues: "'Mommy has gone away. Sometimes in the world, daddies go away and mommies bring up their little boys. But sometimes a mommy can go away, too, and you have your daddy to bring you up. I have gone away because I must find something interesting to do for myself in the world. Everybody has to, and so do I.'"

Now Billy is staring vacantly at the television.

"'Being your mommy was one thing . . . but there are other things, too. And this is what I have to do. I did not get a chance to tell you this, and that is why I am writing you now. I will always be your mommy, and I will always love you. I just won't be your mommy in the house; but I'll be your mommy of the heart. And now . . .'"

Billy starts turning up the sound on the television, drowning out his father's voice.

"We're going to read this another time," says Ted, folding the letter.

"I don't care," replies Billy.[12]

Ibsen's Nora left her husband and children to "find some opening," and Joanna Kramer left her husband and children to find "something interesting to do" in California—trying to redefine themselves, they both turned to a job. Work as the answer to self-actualization is a theme echoing throughout literature and the history of women's activism.

The problem without a name is as old as time: it is the quest for identity, meaning, and purpose. There's nothing new under the sun. The quest is an age-old pursuit; money is just a way of keeping score. But as women, too many of us have bought and taken Friedan's prescription, only to become mothers in the middle and discover that we've thrown the babies out with the *dishwater*. That self-actualization is a vacant, empty shell if it comes at the expense of our children.

What makes finding answers so difficult is that there are in fact women who have much in common with Nora and Joanna. Both were in desperate straits; they had indeed lost their identities.

It is precisely that loss, multiplied thousands of times over in countless dollhouses, that became one of the contributing factors in the feminine identity crisis that Friedan wrote about. Ironically, the greatest legacy of Friedan's prescription is that her feminine mystake has further devalued mothers and motherhood—and thereby women—in the pursuit of uplifting womanhood.

What so many of us believed would cure our basic identity crisis has created another one and left us caught—true mothers in the middle. We've swallowed the feminine mystake and have been chasing after self-actualization, only to discover that we're running toward the wrong goal. And that by making the chase for the almighty dollar in the workplace our measurement of success, we may be—as we'll see in the next chapter—playing on the wrong field.

Three

Playing on the Wrong Field

What would women be like if they were free
to develop without being pressured to conform
to some pattern set by men?

Miriam Schneir[1]

Remember Victoria? She's the mother of two who said she feels as if there were "a big black line drawn through the middle of me." She elaborated on that idea by telling us:

"My job makes it inordinately difficult to have balance between work and home. I guess if [my company] had wanted me to have children, they would have given them to me, you know.

"My husband and I have been working on how we achieve balance. George has finally found it in his career. So now that we have more than enough income, the question at hand is, *How can Victoria become more of a presence in the children's lives?* We're not having any more kids, and they're not getting any younger. They are starting to realize that Dad's around more than Mom is, and they want Mom to be here for this and that.

"I'm at a crossroads about how to make my career work for my family. Because, real honestly, it's almost as if there's something missing—the career is so demanding. You take a day off and you are three times behind. I'm in an industry that is just plagued with human resource issues—constantly. I have about ten thousand people working for me, so the problems never stop. It's tough to manage even the most urgent priorities at work and still make sure that every week there is time set aside to do something with the kids and be an integral part of their lives.

"Even though I try so hard, they get pushed aside an awful lot, and I don't like that. I'm a very organized individual and I'm struggling with it—so I can't imagine how others cope.

"I don't have weekends off—only Sundays. It's six days a week and I travel and I'm never home on Friday nights; I'm expected to be out in the field on Friday nights, because that's when the bulk of our work occurs. I'm also required to work with every one of our ten area managers for a full day in a region that covers a big chunk of the Midwest.

"So when you start to plug those sheer time and travel numbers into the equation, there aren't a whole lot of days left where Mommy leaves at eight and Mommy comes home at five and sits down at the dinner table with the family.

"That's the dilemma I'm in today. If you look at the other female executives in our company, they are single, divorced, married with no children, or their children are grown. I'm the only one who is rearing children and doing this job."

Sylvia attended an Ivy League university. She met her husband, Larry, in college; they married and moved to New York City immediately after graduation. She hit Madison Avenue, while he took on Wall Street—the consummate power couple. Her own combination of ability, drive, and personality kept propelling her upward in her company.

Sylvia worked for four years before they had their first daughter. Pregnancy was not a big deal for her, so she just kept right on going. Her life seemed almost seamless—she found a fabulous nanny to care for her daughter in their home, and she was promoted into a senior position, one level below partner.

But then the seams started to fray. Two years later they had another daughter, and the guilt started to plague her. *Am I doing the right thing by staying here?* she asked herself. *Am I neglecting my kids?*

Then they had a third child, a son, and the seams came undone.

"After seven years with my company, I realized my life was out of whack. I'd reached a breaking point, because I was trying to give 110 percent to kids, husband, home, and work—never necessarily in that order. I just couldn't do it. I would get bouts of bronchitis. I'd be down for three weeks. Of course, I never stayed home from work that long.

"I was wearing myself to the bone, because I want to be an A+ player in everything I do. And I just couldn't do it. I either had to be a mediocre player at work or a mediocre mom and a mediocre wife. I wasn't willing to settle for that. I decided that something in my life had to give."

There is no doubt that feminism has enabled more and more women like Victoria and Sylvia to pursue challenging and fulfilling careers and to succeed in attaining significant positions and power. And that is good.

But with that success has come new questions of identity, and unprecedented pressures on women in the workplace. And the fast-track women executives aren't the only ones who feel it. The issue impacts every mother in the middle. And yet no one seems willing to address the basic problem: how does motherhood fit in?

Just prior to the 1995 United Nations World Conference on the Rights of Women, Betty Friedan wrote an article for *Newsweek* in which she outlined an "updated" vision for feminism. In it she said that we need a "new paradigm of social policy. . . . There has to be some new vision of community. . . . We need to reframe the concept of success." Indeed we do. And yet she goes on to conclude that "the basis of women's empower-ment is economic—that's what is in danger now."[2]

Friedan didn't begin to address the real-life concerns of Victoria and Sylvia. Neither did she answer other questions that mothers in the middle need to be asking: How does stress-ing economic empowerment reframe the concept of success? Is that really how we want to use our power? Could we be playing on the wrong field? Have we been playing by the wrong rules since the beginning?

The Seneca Falls Declaration of 1848 was the first formal American statement of women's rights—it gave form and sub-stance to the burgeoning feminist movement. Nowhere does it mention motherhood (though that may be more of a reflec-tion of a universal acceptance of motherhood's importance at the time than it was a sign the delegates considered the subject too insignificant to raise).

However, at the very last of the convention, as an adden-dum, Lucretia Mott stepped forward and added this final resolution:

> Resolved, That the speedy success of our cause depends upon the zealous and untiring efforts of both men and women . . . for the securing to women an equal participation with men in the various trades, professions, and commerce.[3]

Today feminism's ongoing discussion of this same, as-yet-unrealized goal revolves around two contemporary words: "glass ceiling." Everywhere we turn in discussions about women's needs, those words are repeated like a mantra. *Glass ceiling. Glass ceiling.* But let's just imagine for a moment that the ceiling is broken and women begin swarming into corpo-rate boardrooms until the magical fifty percent representa-tion—Mott's "equal participation"—is achieved.

What would we have won?

Would that be success?

Lucretia Mott was not a materialist: she was a devout Quaker minister and mother of six—a woman who became a leader of the suffrage movement as an outgrowth of her work against slavery. Her home was a stop on the Underground Railroad, and Frederick Douglass described her as "a glorified presence, bearing a message of light and love."[4] Nevertheless, "the success of our cause," after achieving the vote, became synonymous with workplace equality.

But is that real success? Where is the "radical" agenda in that? Is trying to break the glass ceiling really revolutionary?

What happened to Ibsen's Nora and Joanna Kramer when they pursued work as the answer to their identity problems? Did they find success? We can only try to imagine what happened to Nora—*A Doll's House* ends with Nora slamming the door behind her. But Joanna, true to real life, discovers that success in the workplace doesn't mean a whole lot without her son. (She ends up making more money than Ted! And ironically, he loses his job under the pressures of combining fatherhood with his job—highlighting just how difficult it is to do both.)

The truth is that with rare exceptions, corporate careers are not infused with meaning. In fact, they are often banal. Several years ago journalist Liz Gallese studied the women from the Harvard Business School class of 1975 and wrote *Women Like Us*. While reviewing the book, Barbara Ehrenreich retells the story of Phoebe. Phoebe's "moment of glory at Harvard Business School" came when she gave an analysis concluding that Smucker's should never switch to a wide-mouthed ketchup container because people like the challenge of pounding ketchup out of a bottle. Ehrenreich asks, "Is this what we left the kitchen for?"[5] Indeed.

Of course, men have always had to face the banality of their work. That's not exactly the point.

More and more women are conflicted not over having left the kitchen but over having left their children. Certainly the challenges of selling ketchup or Alka-Seltzer might compete with scrubbing out a sink or a stove, but for the mother in the middle, it's not the kitchen she misses but the thrill of watching a child's first steps and the joy of teaching a baby to say, "Mama."

Children As the Impediment

In the century and a half since Seneca Falls, as more and more women and mothers have left home for the highways and byways of business, commerce, and industry, they've run into a major roadblock that feminism has long tried to ignore. It wasn't a glass ceiling.

What the feminists didn't account for was children.

The Industrial Revolution that played such an integral role in drawing women into the workplace simultaneously attempted to replace them at home. There were machines now to make the clothes, and stores to sell bread and milk—so much of women's domestic production was taken over by technology. Yet there was no machine that could mind their children. What technology could replace a mother's cool hand on a fevered forehead?

Children, as every mother in the middle knows, always have been—and forever will be—labor intensive.

Sue Shellenbarger, the work-and-family reporter for the *Wall Street Journal*, had to discover for herself that mothering is one job that defies a technological or programmatic replacement:

> Before I had kids, I once criticized a colleague for staying home because his two children were sick. Annoyed that work was piling up in the news bureau we comanaged, I asked him, "Can't you just put your kids in one of those hospital programs?" He shot me a disgusted look and stomped out of my office. I was puzzled at his response to what I thought was sensible advice. . . .

A year after I criticized my coworker, I had a baby myself. A few months later I missed work, because she was sick. As I explained my absence, the same coworker grinned and asked, "Can't you just put your kid in one of those hospital programs?"

"No way!" I gasped. Then, remembering my own advice to him two years earlier, I briefly considered crawling under my desk as he exited my office, laughing.[6]

Sue can be forgiven her boorishness for one very good reason: she was merely reflecting the values and attitudes she had absorbed from contemporary society. Work is the top priority; children can take care of themselves.

Child care has become, in the world's eyes, a small thing. It's a harsh judgment to bring to daylight, but the underlying assumption is that women of real talent would be squandering their abilities to be "only" mothers. That judgment in turn is based on a value system that no longer values children. Motherhood is not valued simply because children are not.

It was a very large and important gathering. Hundreds of people had come to hear the famous lecturer speak. He was to address some of the most important issues of the day, so a subsequent debate had been arranged with a group of religious leaders. All the local dignitaries were present; it was a very impressive event.

Some of the parents of the community hoped their children would have a chance to meet the great man. They knew that if they did, it would be an experience to treasure the rest of their lives. A few even brought babies. Unfortunately, in their own inimitable way, the babies and small children made their presence known. It was an unwelcome disruption, and the speaker's assistants rushed to chastise the parents and reestablish order and decorum to the event.

The commotion caught the attention of the speaker, just as his assistants had feared. He was indignant.

But not, to everyone's surprise, at the parents or the children.

The keynote speaker stopped in the middle of the important debate with the religious leaders and motioned to the children to come out of the shadows and up to the front. "Let the little children come to me," he said.

All the assembled dignitaries then stood around waiting impatiently to get back to the important issues they had been debating, while the great man focused on each and every child. "Do not hinder them," he said, "for the kingdom of God belongs to such as these."[7]

Jesus apparently thought the children were more important than the adult work he had come to do that day.

Children of the Shadows

This horrified reaction to a child's disruptive presence is familiar to any parent who has tried to take a child out of their separate, shadowy suburban world and into the adult sphere. Children are simply not "in context." The work world is where the sun shines.

It wasn't always this way. When work , home, and child rearing were more integrated, children were also more integrated into the society. Children were a central feature of life, and as a result, entertainment and adult life were more child centered, even childish. Adult recreation did not always require a baby-sitter, as it does now. All of life was more seamless.

Anne Dally, in her book *Inventing Motherhood: The Consequences of an Ideal*, tells us:

> Children in our society are kept away not only from the world of work but also from many adult pleasures and leisure activities, particularly outside the family. Although there are places and activities which

whole families can enjoy together, one cannot take young children to the cinema, bingo hall, betting shop, pub, or golf course. In a simpler, preindustrial society, pleasure as well as work tended to involve the whole community. Adults and children all participated. It was not necessary to separate the children along with those who mothered them. Adult pleasures were more childish than they are today, and children's pleasures were more like those of adults. Children played bowls, card games, and games of chance for money. Adults played games that today would be considered childish, such as leapfrog, bowling hoops, and fighting with snowballs. Children also took part in seasonal activities which were important in the life of the whole community, such as folk dancing and dancing round the maypole.[8]

As Sue Shellenbarger's experience illustrates, often it takes having children to value them. Today many people have little or no contact with children at all and just as little appreciation for them.

Just ask any mother of a large family (anyone with more than three children) what kind of reaction she gets whenever someone learns how many children she has.

———————————————

Rebecca, one mother of seven, told us:

"We get a zillion comments about our children—not about their behavior but about the size of our family. It's comments like, 'Why would you want all those kids?'

"I remember when I just had the older four and would take them shopping. People would actually walk up and stop me—every time I went out—to ask, 'Are all those children yours?' I was always tempted to say, 'No, I went all around the neighborhood and gathered up loose children, because it is so much fun to take them shopping!'

"What irritated me even more were the frequent questions like, 'Don't you know what causes that?' or 'Can't you prevent that?' The assumption is always that we didn't want these children. Or that we shouldn't want these children.

"I didn't realize that people would be that concerned about the size of *our* family. I thought it was a personal decision. Evidently it's not. At least, not after the third child.

"When you have a big family, you get an eye-opening exposure to society's view of children. They aren't valued today."

Boring Blobs

The media often reflects the same opinion.

An article entitled "Great! Now My Friend's a Mom-to-Be—But Is She Still My Friend?" in *Cosmopolitan* is a perfect example: the tongue-in-cheek tone of the article is used as a thin disguise for the anti-baby message. "Of course I felt angry, alienated," writes Charlotte Latvala, the author. "The woman was deserting me for an illiterate, eight-pound blob."

Latvala goes on to list the six stages a friend of a pregnant woman goes through. The first is denial: "In the beginning, most people simply refuse to believe the effect a baby—which, after all, is human only in the strictly scientific sense of the word—will have on a friendship." Second is anger, then alienation: "Try to distance yourself from your friend's happiness." Fourth is acceptance. Fifth, the birthday. Finally, sixth is "The End," at which point Latvala counsels that you can adjust in several ways. But eventually, she points out, you will most likely have your own baby and have something in common again. She concedes that this is a great solution with one major drawback: "You must give up your life and become the kind of person you've been complaining about for years."[9]

Children are the impediment—why waste time caring for a blob? A really happening, Cosmo woman of the nineties would be better off targeting the glass ceiling. Articles like this one are being read by young women in their early twenties, who are the mothers of the next century. The underlying message—that children are not valued—while left at the subliminal level (or in Latvala's case, clothed in a cynical attempt at humor) for deniability's sake, is still not lost on women.

Just in case we miss the message and persist in an unreasoning attachment to the sentimental ideal of motherhood, the general culture can be counted on to reinforce and deliver the theme. We'll get the message elsewhere . . . and everywhere. Self-actualization is the goal; work is the game; children are an impediment. Babies, don't you know, are *boring* blobs.

Faye and Walter have a little girl, Brittany, who just turned two. Faye is a neurosurgical nurse practitioner who works two days a week. Before Brittany was born, Faye planned to return to work full-time after her four-month maternity leave. But when the time came to go back, Faye stretched her leave out to seven months.

"I just thought it was too soon and she was too little for me to go back. . . . It was so hard," said Faye. Finally Faye gave up entirely the idea of going back full-time.

Faye is very happy—especially because her nursing career allows her the flexibility to maintain her professional experience part-time.

But she still remembers one neurosurgeon's comments about her pregnancy. He wanted to know when she would be returning from maternity leave. Then he continued editorially, "You could never be a stay-at-home mom," he said. "You'd be so bored."

Are children really boring? The pro-workplace propagandists sure want to reinforce that idea to the mother in the middle. Another *Cosmopolitan* author and subscriber to the stay-at-home-mom mirage, Carol Lawson, wrote "Don't Let the Guilt Get to You." According to Lawson, the children of at-home moms "do not see them as role models who are connected to the larger world. In truth, these moms have little to talk about other than their kids, and more than one has complained to me, 'I am bored.'"

Apparently, Lawson herself is busy avoiding boredom. She tells the story of racing from the office to the nursery school to make it to her daughter's third birthday party. The teacher asked Lawson, as the mother of the birthday girl, to stay and read a story to the class at the conclusion of the party. Lawson decided instead to rush back to her office. Two years later her daughter still asks sometimes, "Mommy, why did you leave my party?"

She then recounts another story of a mom whose four-year-old daughter announced, "You have to stop working. I need a mother." The article consoled, "You may not be there all day, but you *are* a good mommy. Read this reassuring report and feel *better*"[10] (emphasis theirs). Shades of Joanna Kramer, and the mommy of the house vs. the mommy of the heart.

The conclusion, of course, is this: don't let the guilt get to you. Because, after all, the baby is human only in the strictly scientific sense of the word. Children are the impediment to our self- actualization, because they are *booorrring*. Boredom we must avoid at all costs.

Beyond the Glass Ceiling

Is there a possibility, however remote, that life beyond the glass ceiling is not self-actualized, either? Is there a chance that the glass ceiling acts as a prism, distorting our view of the occupants behind it? Is it conceivable that few people—male or female—shatter the glass ceiling without getting cut?

A recent issue of the *Wall Street Journal* profiled one of America's fifty most powerful women managers. She manages a staff of twenty and oversees more than $250 million in pension assets for a major investment firm. The article detailing her impressive professional success was entitled "Success at a Huge Personal Cost." The reporter notes, however, that this successful female executive is "matter-of-fact" about her sacri-fices—"a first marriage, time with her son, a suburban home, a second child."

The woman's husband, who is a chief investment officer for another firm, has five children from another marriage, two of whom are still at home. They have two nannies to care for the children. But even with all that care available, her seven-year-old son announced to the school nurse, "I haven't eaten in three weeks."

When his mother asked him why he said it, the boy responded, "I just felt that way." And then his true feelings came out when he pleaded with her, "Don't travel so much."[11]

Is life beyond the glass ceiling "success?" G. K. Chesterton, in discussing men and success, once made the point that it is easy to hide individual failure behind the facade of group accomplishment:

> In the problem of private versus public life there is another neglected truth ... anything on a grand scale gives the illusion of a grand success. Curiously enough, multiplication acts as a concealment. Repeti-tion actually disguises failure.
>
> Take a particular man, and tell him to put on a particular kind of hat and coat and trousers and to stand in particular attitudes in the back garden; and you will have great difficulty persuading yourself (or him) that he has passed through a triumph and trans-figuration. Order four hundred such hats, and eight hundred such trousers, and you will have turned the fancy costume into a uniform. Make all the four hun-dred men stand in the special attitudes on Salisbury Plain, and there will rise up before you the spirit of a regiment. Let the regiment march past, and, if you

have any life in you above the brutes that perish, you will have an overwhelming sense that something splendid has just happened, or is just going to begin....

It is not really possible to know the characters of all the four hundred men in the marching column as well as one might know the character of the one man attitudinizing in the back garden. *If all the four hundred men were individual failures, we could still vaguely feel that the whole thing was a success. If we know the one man to be a failure, we cannot think him a success.*[12] (Emphasis ours.)

Is this not what has happened beyond the glass ceiling? The group stands together in their gray custom-made suits and fine silk ties, fortified by their imposing desks, protected by their officious secretaries. They break away from the pack to appear on the covers of *Forbes* and *Fortune*. *Vanity Fair* chronicles them as a group, the New Establishment. Surely, this is what success looks like. Most important, beyond the glass ceiling they aren't bored.

Who are these men (and a handful of women) whom so many are desperately trying to join beyond the glass ceiling in their pursuit of self-actualization? A few of them may be mothers in the middle, still struggling like Victoria and Sylvia to balance work and family responsibilities. But far too often, they are the modern-day "robber barons" who have left behind the wreckage of a failed marriage and family life. (Indeed, the rise of the "trophy wife" has become so prominent that *Fortune* put the trend on its cover, and Olivia Goldsmith hit the *New York Times* best-seller list with her funny but tragic book *The First Wives Club*.)

And these are the people writing the rules of The Game?

Time-out for a Sports Analogy

Suppose for a moment we could arrange an afternoon of competition between Michael Jordan and Greg Maddux. Jordan is considered by many to be the greatest basketball player in history, while Maddux is the only baseball player ever to win the Cy Young Award—given to the league's best pitcher each year—four seasons in a row.

The games begin with a little half-court one-on-one. Who would you bet on? No contest! Maddux wouldn't stand a chance.

But then we move on to the baseball field, with Maddux on the mound and Jordan at bat. Now who wins? Again, no contest. Most of Michael's swings give new meaning to the term "Air Jordan."

Both Jordan and Maddux are known for their competitive natures, their physical conditioning, their natural gifts and instincts, and their work ethic, which have resulted in finely polished and practiced athletic skills. Their athletic performances are often compared to things of beauty. Each is arguably the best ever at what he does.

However, even the most exceptional professional athletes often can't compete in a second sport. Those few who do are notably unusual—as Michael Jordan himself learned when he failed to get past baseball's minor leagues.

What is the game in today's society? Success. And it is, by and large, a male game. And that's certainly nothing new.

"A woman," wrote Ibsen in explaining *A Doll's House*, "cannot be herself in contemporary society; it is an exclusively male society with laws drafted by men, and with counsel and judges who judge feminine conduct from the male point of view."[13] A century later, even though there are now legislators, counsels, and jurists who are women, that judgment still rings true. Does it have to be that way?

Feminist writer Miriam Schneir says that the central question of feminism has been, *"What would women be like if they were free to develop without being pressured to conform to some pattern set by men?"*[14] And yet feminism seems to have completely capitulated to the male game. They have been fighting for women to be "accepted" on men's terms instead of on their own terms.

Women today are playing ball on the male field: some are doing well; others are not. Either way, we're running toward the wrong goal.

An Echo of Men?

"Success" in our society today has been defined, largely, by a masculine model. You are your career; the workplace is the field; the paycheck is the goal line. Success, for men *and* women, has been misdefined as economic accomplishment, and so we've lost the biblical standard of requiring people to be good parents in order to be considered successful.

It is not that work is wrong—success is a good thing! There's no need to say that we should all be ascetic monks. Nor are women dolls. It is just that the game has been written in such a way that it often does not allow for good parenthood for either men or women.

Doug Sokolosky, a former IBM executive, is now a consultant who specializes in coaching women who want to make a run at the top. Among his materials is the following advice:

> *Violate the unwritten rules at your peril.* Unwritten rule No. 1: To reach the top requires sacrifice and long hours. If that's your ambition, forget things like balancing work and family.[15]

"Every corporation says it's trying to accommodate women through things like flextime," Mr. Sokolosky says. "The truth is, when you close the door and say, 'Who's going to run the next region?' those kinds of things come into the decision making."[16]

Women have succeeded in getting in the game, but it is indeed those unwritten rules that direct our plays. Acknowledging this, the Harvard Women's Law Association, in their guide for young, aspiring female attorneys, says, "Act like a man and time your pregnancies appropriately." But again, children aren't welcome no matter what sex the parent: the guide tells of two male associates who were "so afraid to leave work that they didn't join their wives in the delivery room when their children were born."[17]

Saying that women are trying to play the male game can be misinterpreted. We certainly don't want to fall into the dangerous dualism that prescribes a separate male sphere of work and an isolated female sphere that assigns child care exclusively to women: children need both their parents. And tragically, the devaluing of motherhood is just a piling-on after the demise of the cultural prototype that David Blankenhorn, in *Fatherless America*, calls the "good family man."[18] Our work-family arrangements, The Game, don't work well for mothers *or* fathers.

Katherine Hudson is one woman who smashed the glass ceiling into a million pieces: she is the CEO of W. H. Brady. In a forum discussion about women at the top, with other CEOs and former U.S. Secretary of Commerce Barbara Hackman Franklin, Brady commented, "Women have spent thirty years learning how to 'make it in a man's world.' The problem is that the guy's world is flawed."[19]

The good family man is a man who "puts his family first." And in our society, Blankenhorn points out, he is increasingly rare.

Will the good mother join hands with her mate and be drawn into the game ... or will she draw him toward higher priorities? Parenthood (for men and women) needs regeneration in our society.

But this is a book about mothers, because the heavier child-care burden inevitably falls to them. There *is* a biological imperative that brings the mother into greater involvement with her babies. So if women do not value their children, why would men? As Chesterton points out, "We cannot insist that the first years of infancy are of supreme importance, and that mothers are not of supreme importance; or that motherhood is a topic of sufficient interest for men, but not of sufficient interest for mothers."[20]

The Zen of Motherhood

The sad irony in all this is that motherhood is anything but boring. But like most challenging tasks, it is sufficiently interesting only insofar as it is attended to. Like anything involving relationships, successful motherhood is achieved over time and through perseverance.

The wonder of parenthood reveals itself in small moments. Unfortunately, many of today's mothers in the middle don't slow down long enough to make that discovery. Others simply don't have the opportunity.

As a single career woman, Iris Krasnow flew higher than most: she was the Washington feature writer for United Press International, a job that took her to "eating cheeseburgers with Billy Graham in New York City, smoking Camel nonfilters with Yoko Ono at the Dakota, munching peanuts with Queen Noor at her palace in Amman." Not an easy career to trade in for diapers.

But she did it. At forty years old, Iris found herself at home with four boys under the age of five—the last two twins.

She had been the classic baby boomer searching after self-actualization. In her Stanford days, she says, "My identity shifted with the semesters, with the ever-changing Bay Area trends. In my quest to make sense of who I was, I was hypnotized. I did EST. I lived in a white Ford supervan along the Big Sur ocean cliffs. Enlightenment came, but it was fleeting."

Her work, with all its glamour and prestige, somehow never filled the empty place inside. "At the core of my success," she says, "was a gnawing emptiness."

But motherhood was different. An emptiness that had been so huge, that was not filled up even by large accomplishments, suddenly vanished in the face of something small and seemingly insignificant: the everyday life of babies.

"With the birth after birth of son after son, I have moved beyond the wrenching self-analysis that had forever rocked my core. Today I am enmeshed in a world of little things and little people, of being slammed into the moment with such ferocity and velocity that now is all there is. My kids have captured me and I have surrendered. I am no longer mine; I am theirs."

Funny thing. In losing herself, she found her self.

"I once loved to try to decipher my own self and its relation to God and the universe. Dulled by too little sleep and too many children, I lack the motive to keep wallowing in the search. Wallowing takes brainpower, soul power, time. And frankly, all that thinking in a corner doesn't get you anywhere. It's the perpetual motion of kids that zaps you into truth.

"Now, in the Zen of motherhood, I have finally discovered a lasting joy in the fleetingness of life. As four tiny bodies lie wedged like puppies between my husband and me on our king-sized bed, I know in my heart that life, however frenetic and mindless, is hopeful and sweet. The relentless climb is over, at least for now. It was at the top of the mountain that the true self came knocking, and I found my way home."[21]

What is the truth? One truth is that motherhood is a challenge unlike any other in life—and done rightly, it takes every fiber of our being and gives back even more. The return on investment of motherhood has eternal significance. What does The Game return? Economic empowerment? Is that success?

The pursuit of self-actualization in the workplace is a pathetic mimicry of the mistake men have made for centuries.

In 1888 Elizabeth Cady Stanton, a true pioneer, told the International Council of Women, "Thus far women have been the mere echoes of men. . . . The true woman is as yet a dream of the future."[22]

One hundred and eight years later the true woman still sleeps. Our voices crying out, "Break the glass ceiling!" at the edge of a canyon bounce back sounding impressive but then ricochet off, traveling down the mountains, dissipating into nothingness.

From the shadows, does anyone hear, "*Look at me!*"?

Four

The Ultimate Value
of Motherhood

*The love most adults feel for a
newborn child is totally irrational.
There is no way to describe it in the language of choice,
the language of individual self-interest,
or the language of cost-benefit.*

Barbara Dafoe Whitehead[1]

Denise and Rob were married a month after their high
school graduation. Rob went to work at his father's lumber store. Denise took a job as a cashier at a department store.
Three years later, just months before the birth of their first
child, Rob confided in Denise that his father's once-successful
business was floundering, that his father had taken some ill-
advised business risks, and the company was on the verge of
bankruptcy.

As he told Denise, Rob began to cry. He had always loved
going to the store with his father as a child. He loved the smell
of freshly sawed wood and the feel of a power saw in his
hands. Rob's father had always told him, "The store will be
yours when I am gone." Rob had been sure that running the
lumber store was what he wanted to do with his life.

Now Rob wondered how long he would have a job. He had no idea what else he wanted to do. His father had made him a junior partner last year. Would that make him financially liable for his father's debts? How would he, Denise, and the baby make ends meet if his father lost the store? Neither Rob nor Denise knew.

Then, less than a month before the baby was due, Rob's mother separated from his father and filed for divorce.

When Denise and Rob talked about this latest development in their lives, Rob commented, "I had hoped you could stay home with the baby for a while."

Denise laughed, "Women don't do that anymore. I'd be bored stiff at home with a baby!"

Being practical, they both agreed that they could hardly give up their only stable income: Denise's pay.

Then their baby son arrived. Denise told us:

"Before Robby was born, I guess I worried some about childbirth and whether or not he would be OK. But our lives were so wrapped up in Rob's family problems! That overshadowed everything else. I ended up being almost surprised by the baby.

"When Robby was born, all I could see, all I could think about, was how wonderful he was. Even then, in those first moments, I could see how he looked like Rob, with his mouth and jaw. And like my father, through the eyes.

"His skin was so soft and smelled so good. I just fell in love with him.

"Since I was planning to go back to work, I didn't want to start breast-feeding. But I loved holding him while I gave him his bottle.

"The first few weeks at home were exhausting! Robby had me up three or four times every night. I was always tired. I kept burning the bottle nipples when I sterilized them. One evening, Rob came home from work and I was still in a bathrobe with baby spit-up down the front.

"Yet even though it was hard, I felt glad that when Robby cried, I was the one he was crying for. I was surprised that within a week or so, I could tell why he was crying. I could tell Rob, 'That's his hungry cry' or 'That's his my-diaper-needs-changing cry.' And I would be right.

"I'd never been much of a 'baby person.' But when Robby was awake, I would sit and hold him and look at his eyes. I'd try to decide how he looked like me—not much!—and how he looked like other family members. And I talked to him all the time, telling him how cute he was and how much we loved him.

"I amazed myself at how goo-goo silly I was about this baby! And I wondered, *Why didn't anybody tell me motherhood would be so intense?* I was falling in love with my son. And watching Rob with Robby, I fell in love with my husband all over again.

"Robby was only a month old when he had his first ear infection. When he woke up crying that night, I knew that something was wrong. That it was more than his 'hungry' or 'diaper' cry. The antibiotic for his ear infection gave him diarrhea, which resulted in awful diaper rash. So I learned his 'earache' cry and his 'my-bottom-is-raw' cry.

"When Robby was five weeks old, we stopped and visited the day care center where I had signed him up. I wanted to give him a chance to see it before he started the following week.

"I had liked the place a lot when I had visited during my pregnancy. Now, with Robby in my arms, I was looking with different eyes.

"They had two teachers in the room, with eight babies. That had seemed like enough before. But now I knew how hard it was for me with only one baby. *How did anybody handle four babies?* I looked at the teachers and realized that they weren't the same women who had been there when I signed up. I asked the director and found out that both teachers were new; the old ones had left the center 'for personal reasons.' And of course, since he would be at the center from 8:00 a.m. until 5:00 p.m., different teachers would be with him at the end of the day.

"I went home really depressed. That day care center was supposed to be the best in town. But how could I leave Robby there? How would all those different teachers know when his cry was 'hungry' and when it was his diaper, or when he was beginning to get sick? Would they talk to him? I hadn't seen them talking to the babies when we visited. I hadn't thought of any of those things before Robby was born.

"But I had no choice. We needed my money. And a part of me was ready to get out of the house and back into the real world. Let someone else change his diaper and feed him his bottle. It would be nice to have time to take a shower and dress like a regular person.

"My first few weeks back at work were horrible. Robby was still up several times a night—so I was, too. One of my coworkers quit. My boss kept wanting me to work overtime. I'd always been willing to do that before. But now overtime meant less time with Robby. And every morning, trying to get to work on time was miserable. I was so tired! It took a month before we began to settle into something of a routine.

"Then, one week when Robby was three months old, our whole world turned upside down.

"Rob's worst fears about the family business came true when he learned his dad wouldn't be able to meet the mid-month payroll.

"And at the beginning of that same week, one of Robby's teachers quit, and at the end of the week, another one did, too. 'For personal reasons' again. My first contact with one of the new teachers was when she called to tell me Robby was sick and could I pick him up?

"My boss was mad. The store was short handed and he didn't want me to leave. I called Rob, but he was in the middle of yet another crisis at work. When I arrived at the day care, the teacher informed me that they would 'surely appreciate it if I wouldn't bring Robby when he was sick.'

"Was I mad! But I felt guilty too. How could I tell that Robby was sick, when I was never around him to hear his 'sick' cry? He hadn't been running a fever when I'd taken him to day care.

"When Rob came home from work late that night, I told him, 'We can't go on like this anymore!' And he agreed."

The next day, Rob and a family friend sat down with Rob's dad and hammered out a plan to pay off their creditors. And he was able to make payroll, only two days late.

Rob brought the store books home, and he and Denise began sorting out the mess. Denise continued:

"It took us six more months to get the business back on semistable ground. Then Rob and I decided that we needed someone we could trust keeping the books at the store. And who could we trust more than me? So I quit my job and went to work for Rob.

"Then I began to think about Robby. We needed someone we could trust with our son. *Who could we trust more than me? Were the books at the store more important than our son?"*

Denise called Sandra, a friend from high school who'd had a baby girl a month after Robby was born. She found out that Sandra had decided to quit work, stay at home, and keep some children to help out financially. Denise jumped at the opportunity. And within two weeks, Robby was out of the day care center and into Sandra's home.

"I leave Robby with Sandra two days a week and work in the office. But the rest of my work I can do at home, either during naptime or in the evenings while Rob plays with Robby. Sometimes I work after Robby is asleep at night.

"Now I am the one with Robby most of the time. And I love it."

Babies Need Their Mamas

Denise has discovered what most mothers know instinctively but have to affirm with personal experience, and what child development experts confirm through research and study: babies need their mothers.

According to Dr. Fran Stott, dean of the Erikson Institute for Advanced Study in Child Development in Chicago, "Children need more than food, shelter, and clothing. The bottom line is: every child needs at least one person who's crazy about him."[2] That echoes Bronfenbrenner's concept of "mutual, irrational emotional attachment."

Child psychiatrist and infant researcher Stanley Greenspan, in his book *The Essential Partnership*, says:

> Feeling part of a relationship, being fully involved with another person, is an important childhood experience. It is the cornerstone of the child's initial sense of security. It encourages healthy emotional development and helps the child deal with emotional challenges and problems. Especially in the early years, we parents are the perfect partners in this experience. . . .
> For babies to learn about intimacy, for example, requires a responsive, trusted partner who can read the baby's signals for closeness and provide the requested hug. Mechanical, cold holding from one of a sea of faces cannot create the same confidence or security that a warm, tender hug from a valued person does.[3]

Erik Erikson, in his book *Childhood and Society*,[4] calls the issue "trust vs. mistrust." When a baby needs something, he or she cries. If someone responds to the cries and satisfies that need—for food or dry clothing or comfort or whatever—the baby begins to develop a sense of trust. This translates into a feeling of confidence in the world and a sense of power: *If I cry, I have the power to make someone listen to me and meet my needs. And the world must be an OK place, since I get my needs met most of the time.*

The child who cries and cries and gets no response learns to mistrust the world. Or if the baby's cries are often misinterpreted, if no one learns to distinguish between the "hungry" cry and the "my-diaper-needs-changing" cry, if meeting the baby's needs is often postponed, he or she learns that the world can be an unpredictable and uncaring place.

The Connoisseur of People

This process of learning to trust is called attachment. Babies need to have a "secure base" from which they venture out to explore the world. John Bowlby, the psychoanalyst who originated attachment theory, said that babies quickly become "connoisseurs of people."[5] As babies look out at the world, the security of a close bond with their mothers gives them the confidence to grow and develop.

Bowlby's essential point was that in the first few years of life, the human capacity to form relationships and develop intimacy is learned. In order to develop into happy, well-adjusted children, babies must have care that is warm, secure, continuous, and responsive.[6] A growing body of research indicates that the patterns of intimacy and ability to forge bonds with other people which we develop as infants can have lasting effects into adulthood.

Child development researchers studying infant attachment have described four different patterns of behavior that infants develop as a result of their early interactions with their caretakers: the children are either securely attached, anxious-avoidant, ambivalent, or disorganized. The growing evidence that security of attachment influences the behavior of children is impressive. Researcher Jay Belsky, in a review of the attachment data, noted that research has shown:

> Two-year-olds with secure attachment histories were more skilled in solving challenging problems, seeking maternal assistance in the face of challenges, and tolerating frustration.... Three-and-a-half-year-olds with secure attachment histories exhibited, in a nursery school setting, more peer leadership and less social withdrawal and hesitation, greater self-confi-

dence and curiosity about new things, and more sympathy to the distress of others than age-mates judged earlier to be insecure in their relationships with their mothers.[7]

Belsky goes on for several more paragraphs to list the positive benefits of secure attachment for children. Sadly, the converse is also true: research indicates that insecure attachment results in problems for children. Children who are not securely attached are more aggressive, more impulsive, less confident, more dependent, have more behavior problems, and exhibit more antisocial behavior. They are also less sociable, so that by the age of four and five, they are rated by their teachers as less competent with their peers and are less liked by their preschool classmates.[8] A review of the attachment research done for the U.S. Department of Health and Human Services states that:

> Anxiously attached children may be at risk for depression, compulsive caregiving, compulsive self-reliance, agoraphobia, chronic mourning, or milder problems handling anxiety, anger, and intimacy. Extreme avoidance may underlie the sociopath's extreme isolation from his own and others' feelings and needs, including the need for a close personal relationship. Clinical case studies show that a history of anxious attachment often plays a role in psychological disorders.[9]

Belsky points out that a child's development is affected by many factors that must be taken into consideration, including the quality of the parents' marriage, and the levels of stress in a family. But one of the most important factors is maternal employment:

> A number of studies now indicate that children in any of a variety of child care arrangements, including center care, family day care, and nanny care, for

twenty or more hours per week beginning in the first year of life, are at elevated risk of being classified as insecure in their attachments to their mothers at twelve or eighteen months of age and of being more disobedient and aggressive when they are from three to eight years old.[10]

This is essential information for the mother in the middle to know as she makes her own personal choices.

So is the information available? If you see anything at all in the popular literature about attachment, you will probably see it noted that overall, 65 percent of infants exhibit secure attachment.[11] Then it is noted that over half (55 percent) of infants whose mothers work full-time are securely attached.[12] The clear implication is that there is a relatively small difference between the children of mothers who are employed full-time and those whose mothers are not.

Is this true? Only to a point....

What the mother in the middle will never see in the information popularly available to her is what the real difference is: 71 percent of children whose mothers are not employed full-time are classified as securely attached. The true comparison, then, is between the 45 percent of infants whose mothers are employed full-time who are insecure and the 29 percent of infants whose mothers are not employed full-time who are insecure.

The risk, therefore, of insecure attachment for children whose mothers are employed full-time is 55 percent higher— that is to say, the risk is more than one and a half times larger— than for those whose mothers are not working full-time.

Critics often argue that infants do better in high-quality day care. However, as we will discuss more in chapter 8, that is an ideal and does not reflect the real-world choices available to most parents. This attachment data reflects what is actually happening in real-world situations. *The mother in the middle, who is making critical life decisions for her children, deserves to know the truth.*

Mothers are valuable—and the work that they do is essential to the well-being of their children. In a landmark study that he conducted for the World Health Organization in 1951, Bowlby wrote:

> The mothering of a child is not something that can be arranged by roster; it is a live human relationship which alters the characters of both partners. The provision of a proper diet calls for more than calories and vitamins: we need to enjoy our food if it is to do us good. In the same way, the provision of mothering cannot be considered in terms of hours per day but only in terms of the enjoyment of each other's company which mother and child obtain.[13]

Most mothers know intuitively that no one else can do what they can do for their babies. Who else would be crazy enough about a baby to learn the baby's individual cues and respond appropriately? To try and try again to discover why she is crying and rock her, crying with her when all else fails? To offer running commentary on the laundry and grocery shopping, to talk about the sunset and the flowers, to share hopes and dreams for the future, with a small person who cannot talk back? To get up yet one more time in the night to comfort a child who is sick or has had a nightmare? Who can do that job better than (or even as well as) the baby's mother?

The Little Values of a Mother — Did You Know?

- Newborn babies prefer a higher-pitched voice. Not only are most mothers' voices naturally higher than that of a father's but mothers instinctively talk to a newborn in "motherese," a voice pitched higher than their usual voices.
- Immediately after birth, a baby attends longer to the sight of a human face than to anything else.

- A newborn baby moves in rhythm to his mother's voice, enticing his mother to talk to him more.
- Infants recognize, attend to, and are comforted by their mothers' voices within the first week.
- Mothers report being able to distinguish their babies' cries from those of other babies while still in the hospital.
- Babies prefer being rocked head to toe—as in a mother's arms—rather than the back-and-forth rocking of a baby swing.
- By the time a baby is five days old, he recognizes and prefers the smell of his own mother's milk.
- Mother's milk provides specific immunities for her child, against the germs in their particular environment.
- By the time a baby is three to four weeks old, an observer can look at the baby's face, not knowing with whom she is playing, and successfully tell who is interacting with the baby: mother, father, or stranger. With a mother, the baby's movements and facial expressions are smooth and rhythmic, anticipating a calm, low-key interaction. With a father, the baby tenses up, her face lights up, and movements become agitated, in anticipation of father play.

Mothers Need Their Babies

We tend to think about how much a baby needs, gains— or takes—from his or her mother. We often neglect to look at the ways in which mothers benefit from their babies. One mother wrote of her love for her children:

> For many women, the greatest passion they will ever know is for their children. Hints of this surfaced when my daughter was born six years ago. I would marvel at her soft skin, blissfully fall asleep rocking her, and bury my nose is her nape and inhale; no per-

fume in the world could match that scent. And when my son came along twenty months later, those powerful sentiments again ambushed me. . . . I began to talk to other mothers and parent-child experts to plumb the mystery of this affair. The experience, it seems, is, if not universal, certainly widespread.[14]

Babies bring warmth and insecurity, joy and frustration, challenge and growth, into the lives of their mothers. Children push us as mothers to our limits—and beyond—and reward us with a hug and a smile. In doing so, they stretch us. We become better, stronger women.

We talked with nurses who told us that being a mother had broadened their understanding of people and made them better able to care for their patients. Teachers told us how motherhood had given them more insight into and patience for the children in their classes and more empathy with their students' parents. Executives told us how having children had helped make them more sensitive to the personal and professional lives of the people who worked under them. One woman told us that her love for her daughter encouraged her to work on and repair a difficult relationship with her own mother.

Indeed, many women (and men) find that their personal experience as a parent provides a profound sense of appreciation and understanding that deepens and strengthens their relationship with their own mothers and fathers. At the same time that having children reinforces our heritage and gives us insight into our personal pasts, parenthood also connects us to, and prepares us for, the intangible future as we plan and hope and dream for our children's tomorrows.

Many theologians have talked and written about the implications that a personal experience of parental love has on one's understanding of the divine love of God for his earthly children.

We probably need to stop right here and make certain we're not misunderstood. We do not mean to say that being a mother automatically makes a person a better nurse, teacher, or whatever. Neither does it necessarily heal the wounds of dysfunctional families or make mothers more spiritually insightful than other women. And we are certainly not implying that to find happiness, fulfillment, and success in life, a woman has to experience motherhood.

We also want to be clear: not all mothers are good mothers. Some mothers, for a variety of reasons, do not bond immediately with their children, and some not at all. The mother-child relationship, like all relationships, develops over time, with effort, time, and attention.

However, we think it's important to point out, as a counterbalance to any discussion of the costs and the sacrifices involved in motherhood, that the mothers we talked to could point to a long list of ways their lives had been broadened and enriched by their children—lessons they'd learned, insights they'd gained, ways they'd grown and developed and become a better person through their motherhood experience. Which means any discussion of the ultimate value of motherhood shouldn't focus exclusively on the benefits to our children without also acknowledging the benefits (most women we talked to would readily say "greater benefits") we mothers reap from the experience.

The Unique Value of a Mother

Many of the mothers we interviewed told us they had found, rather than lost, a strong sense of their own identity and self-worth in the unique nature of their motherhood roles.

Harriet knew, as early as she can remember, she wanted to have children. Before having children, she worked in the theater, taught swimming, and worked in construction. Harriet told us:

"The day my husband and I first spoke of marriage, I announced very forcefully that when we had children, I wouldn't have someone else raise them. I would be an at-home mom. Fortunately, he agreed.

"Some friends of mine, mothers who work outside the home, felt it was necessary to 'find' me a career. They would say, 'I know what you could be doing with your life.' I finally told them, 'I *am* doing something with my life!'

"Thousands of people can do those other jobs. I am the only person in the whole wide world who can be a mother to my children. I consider putting loving, caring, responsible adults into our world to be a greater accomplishment than anything I could ever do as a high-powered executive of a major company."

Emily doesn't know Harriet, but she would agree with her. Emily worked as an office manager for an insurance company before she had children. She told us:

"I knew I wanted to stay at home with my children. So my life right now *is* my family. I get a lot of fulfillment out of family.

"Maybe when my two boys get older, I can make other choices. I know that there are some things that I would like to do, but I really don't have a desire to do them right now. I want to be with my kids as much as I can.

"I volunteer at the children's school, and I've substitute-taught some. That gives me a chance to know other children and make a little bit of a difference in their lives. We have a construction business we do from our home. I enjoy taking care of the business part of that. And I'm president of the PTA this year.

"I like to be able to pick my boys up from school and to be here for them after school. Later when they are older, maybe in high school, I may look at some other things. But right now I'm doing what I want to be doing. The greatest work I could ever do is raise my children—that's the way I feel. I'm doing my greatest work right now."

Unlike Harriet and Emily, Elizabeth had planned to return to her career after children. Motherhood took her by surprise. She hadn't known that this little person would change her life so. Elizabeth told us:

"Before I had children, I worked as a dental hygienist. We had bought a small house in a nice neighborhood. When we bought the house, we figured I'd have the baby and go back to work. My mother had worked when I was little; everybody I knew worked. It seemed like the thing to do.

"When I had my first child, I stayed home four months, then I went back. I worked full-time for two weeks and decided I just couldn't do it. Then I took vacation time. I went to part-time after I used up my vacation time.

"When I quit even part-time, we moved to a cheaper house in a worse neighborhood. That was a big thing—to move. To get rid of our home. But our new house is decent—it's livable. And to make ends meet, I've had to do home day care. That's really hard at times.

"But every time my kids need a hug, I'm here to give it to them. Their favorite books, they can bring them to me anytime and I can read to them. What if I was at work and they were in day care? Somebody else would be hugging them, if they'd take the time. They'd be reading those books.

"My mother was never home with me as a child. I don't have any memories of her at home. She was always at work. I was a cheerleader and she never came to any of the games. She was always too tired. I can understand that, but I don't want it to be that way for my children. I'd make any sacrifice to be home with them.

"I don't have any regrets."

Torn down the Middle

Victoria, the executive we quoted earlier, talked about her dual roles of mother and career woman by saying, "I feel as if I walk around with a big black line drawn through the middle of me." She isn't alone. Other women have talked to us about feeling divided or torn down the middle by what they saw as conflicting identities—mom and home on one side vs. worker and job on the other.

Dr. T. Berry Brazelton, in his book *Touchpoints*, discusses the grief parents feel as they leave their baby in someone else's care. "When parents turn a baby over to another caregiver, they will feel loneliness, guilt, helplessness, and even anger."[15]

Marney Rich Keenan, the *Detroit News* reporter whose beautiful description of her new-felt mother love we included in chapter 1, talked about returning to her newspaper job after the birth of her daughter. She said:

> "My friends who had gone back to work told me it would be hard. By hard, I though they meant I would feel reluctant, reticent, like going back to school in the fall after summer vacation. . . . I did not expect grief. . . . I did not expect guilt."[16]

Time and again, in our interviews with mothers, this same theme came up: "Why didn't someone tell me that motherhood would be so intense?" Or "I was surprised by how all-consuming my love for my baby was." Or "No one told me leaving my baby would be so hard."

Carol, a social worker, tells her story of going back to work:

"When my son was four months old, I was under contract to go back to work at a mental health clinic working with disturbed children. They really needed me, and breaking the contract would have hurt me professionally. It would have been difficult in the future to get a job. This was only my second year with this clinic.

"Leaving my baby just really hurt. I felt like a victim of going back to work as much as the baby. I actually became physically ill. A sinus infection went into bronchitis, and I ended up being home another three weeks. Looking back, I honestly think that my sickness resulted from just the thought of having to leave the baby.

"Leaving my infant son was one of the hardest things I've ever done. I feel that mothers who go back to work right away have to cut off part of their maternal instinct, a part of their soul."

Marney and Carol are two more mothers in the middle. They once believed the myth that anyone could care for a baby. No one told them how important they would be in the lives of their babies. They did not understand what joy their children would bring to their lives or how hard it would be to leave their babies in someone else's care.

They did not expect to feel grief.

Different but Equal

On February 1, 1995, ABC television ran a one-hour prime-time documentary examining recent research concerning possible biological differences between men and women. In the course of the program, the show's host interviewed the eminent feminist Gloria Steinem and asked whether she thought it possible that women might be born with a unique capacity and potential for nurturing small children. Ms. Steinem's immediate and vehement response was, "*No!* Next question?"

Evidently, Gloria Steinem is ignoring breast-feeding. And she's glibly dismissing a lot more than that.

Over the past three decades, we have been told that men and women are just alike, that women can do anything men can do, that men can do anything women can do. During the same three decades, scientific research has discovered more and more ways in which men and women are different. Our brains are wired differently. We process language and use words differently. We negotiate and handle conflict differently. Men are from Mars; women are from Venus. In a business meeting, a man is a "shark"; a woman is a "dolphin."

According to research, "Women talk to express caring, gain consensus, and build community; men talk to rank one another and maintain a competitive position. . . . The remarkable thing is that these trends are apparent when children first learn to speak."[17]

New research, using brain imagery, actually shows that men and women use different parts of their brains to accomplish the same tasks.[18]

Other research shows that the corpus callosum, the part of the brain that connects the right and left hemispheres of the brain, is larger in women than in men. The difference means that the average woman has millions more neural pathways between the two halves of her brain than the average man does. Scientists theorize that this results in an ability to coordinate right and left brain functions in ways men do not, and may be the basis for "women's intuition."[19]

A growing collection of evidence indicates that men and women are different. Research data strongly support the idea that men and women bring different, complementary skills to the human mix. The question we now face is, How can we place value on both what is uniquely feminine and what is uniquely masculine?

For in trying to eliminate differences, society has devalued the special qualities of both men and women. Nowhere is this clearer than in the arena of motherhood and fatherhood.

Different and Special

Child development experts tell us that mothers and fathers respond to children differently. From the moment of birth, a mother tends to be an "encompasser." She pulls the baby close and holds the baby snugly against her, often instinctively to her left breast so that the baby can hear the comforting sound of her heartbeat.

Fathers, however, tend to be "engrossers." After a baby's birth, the father may try to hold the baby close, but will usually switch to the "en face" position, holding the infant with feet toward his chest, the baby's head cupped in his hand, the father looking into the child's eyes.[20]

Newborns have limited vision that focuses at twelve to fifteen inches—about the distance from the mother's eyes to the baby at her breast. This enables a baby to make eye contact with his mother while he nurses. But this is also the distance at which a father holds a baby "en face."

As a toddler, a child views his or her mother as a "safe haven," venturing out to play but periodically running back to "touch base" with her. She is the one the child runs to for comfort when hurt. Mother play tends to be quieter, calmer: book reading, playing peekaboo or patty-cake, singing, talking.

The father, however, tends to be the parent who whisks the child away to play. Fathers in cultures around the world instinctively toss a baby in the air when the baby is eight to twelve months old—alarming mothers and grandmothers alike. We now know that this activity at this particular age actually stimulates the development of equilibrium in the child's inner ear. And equilibrium is important for learning to walk in the coming months.

Father play is usually rough-and-tumble: swinging the child around, pursuing the child in a wild-animal chase, wrestling and tickling on the floor.

The father tends to be the one who pushes the child toward independence, while the mother tends to be the secure base the child returns to for reassurance.

Children need both.

Many mothers raise children alone and their children grow up to be emotionally happy, well-adjusted adults. Fathers do the same. We certainly do not mean to belittle the parenting skills of those parents. But society does not make their jobs easier by ignoring the fact that mothers and fathers naturally and often instinctively play different, complementary roles in the lives of children.

Why must these differences be considered bad? Sex differences can be viewed as esteem enhancing instead of as a cause for insecurity and feeling inadequate. We would do better to appreciate and celebrate the unique gifts a mother brings to parenting, and the unique gifts brought by a father.

There are countless books that discuss the importance of a mother (or father) in the life of a child. We've only hit the high points in this chapter. Stacks of studies and research affirm the conclusion of world-renowned child development expert Dr. Maria Piers, who in *Growing Up with Children* wrote this about the role of parents:

> They provide him [the child] with the conditions, the necessary mixture of love and frustration, that he needs for the unfolding and development of his innate abilities. To love and also to frustrate—at the right times, in the right measure—is the never-changing task of mother and father, always and everywhere. . . . There is a supporting cast . . . the sitter, the teacher, grandma and grandpa, the doctor, the lady next door . . . they will all help to educate the child. But always his mother is the leading lady, his father the leading man.[21]

If Mama Ain't Happy, Ain't Nobody Happy

The women interviewed for this book, both those who are staying at home with their children and those who are balancing their careers with their young ones, all recognized their importance in the lives of their offspring. These mothers talked about how much they loved their children. They believe that children have enriched their lives. They spoke eloquently of the joy that had come with motherhood.

But their voices spoke also of frustrations.

Women have always worked. And women have always needed support, affirmation, and a sense of productivity. As we spoke with mothers who worked outside the home, they talked about enjoying the camaraderie of the people with whom they worked. Pay raises and promotions, the stimulation of working as part of a team, pride in what they were able to accomplish at work, as well as being able to contribute to the family finances, were counted as the positive side of their jobs.

Yet these were the same women who said things like:

- "I squandered the years when my babies were young."
- "I long to spend more time with my children."
- "I realize that they'll be in school soon and my time with my kids will be over. But I can't see how to be with them more."
- "I'm so tired when I am home, I end up not doing what I want to do with my sons."
- "When I'm with my children, my mind is worrying about my deadline at work."

Mothers at home with their children seemed more happy with their lives, and yet they too expressed frustrations:

- "When my husband is stressed out because of money, I think, *If I had a real job, I could help.*"
- "I wish I weren't so isolated. I wish I didn't have to get into a car and drive who-knows-how-far to get support."
- "My friends who don't have children yet don't understand. They think my life is boring."
- "I felt guilty when my baby was in day care. And now I feel guilty for staying at home and not contributing financially to our family."

These were the voices of women who value their children and long to be the "leading lady" in the life stories of their children but who also want to attend to their own personal needs for productivity, for support, for affirmation. And all are searching for a world in which their work, their needs, and their identities no longer conflict with the needs of their children. All are daily weighing, in their own minds and in their own lives, the ultimate value of motherhood.

These are the mothers in the middle. These are the women caught in the mommy wars.

PART II:

The Mommy Wars

Five

The Battle between the Sexes

*So God created man in his own image . . . male
and female he created them. God blessed them and
said to them, "Be fruitful and increase in number; fill
the earth and subdue it. . . ." God saw all that he had
made, and it was very good.*

Genesis 1:27–31

Stacy met Samuel at college. He was a senior the year that she was a freshman. They got to know each other while attending a rally in support of the Equal Rights Amendment. She liked his offbeat sense of humor and his active commitment to making social changes. Samuel prodded Stacy into thinking about women's issues, about what it meant for her to be a woman, and about what she wanted out of life.

In the four months they dated that year, Stacy fell in love with Samuel. When he ended the relationship, it broke her heart.

Two years passed before they saw each other again. Stacy had taken a summer job in a large city. Imagine her surprise when she bumped into Samuel in a shopping mall after work one day! She hadn't known he lived there, too.

What began as a lunch date to catch up on old memories soon rekindled their romance. They were married the day after Stacy graduated from college. Their marriage, they promised each other in the wedding vows, would be a partnership of equals.

Stacy took Samuel's last name and hyphenated it with her maiden name. They settled in the city where they had met the summer before. Samuel continued his job as a high school teacher. Stacy got a position as a legal assistant at a small law firm.

In the first eight years of their marriage, they took turns going to graduate school. Samuel earned his masters and took a position as a college instructor at a nearby junior college. When Stacy graduated from law school, she became an associate in the firm where she'd first worked as a legal assistant.

During those years, they did laundry together, worked in the yard together, shopped for groceries together. They talked about their roles and worked on mutually agreeable solutions. Their rule of thumb was this: each one did those jobs that mattered most to him or her.

It bothered Stacy that Samuel's idea of something being "clean" around the house didn't seem very clean or even sanitary to her. Samuel's solution was that if she needed for something to be cleaner, if that mattered to her, she needed to be the one to clean it. Since Samuel's standards for cleanliness and clutter were much lower than Stacy's, slowly but surely Stacy took on more and more of the housework.

That seemed to be a small problem, though, in a happy marriage.

Until Stacy found out she was pregnant. While Stacy was hesitant about motherhood at first, Samuel was thrilled. She had received her promotion to junior partner just the year before and really enjoyed the challenge of her profession. No problem, Samuel said. He was burned out as a college professor. Stacy made more money than he did anyway. He'd quit his job and take care of the baby. He'd developed an interest in

rare and collectible books. If he started a used-book-store business, he could take the baby to work with him and schedule
his hours to suit parenthood.

Before the baby arrived, Stacy was happy with that
arrangement. However, when their daughter, Rebecca, was
born, she was overcome with maternal instincts she hadn't
been prepared for. Going back to her office when Rebecca was
six weeks old was the hardest thing she had ever done.

But she and Samuel had an understanding. She felt obligated to live up to it. And somehow her maternal feelings didn't
seem to fit in with her ideals as a feminist. Women today went
back to work when their babies were six weeks old. Why was
she having such a hard time with it? She decided that she
needed to just cope with it.

Samuel, on the other hand, felt as if he had been set free
from his old, frustrating job. Caught up in the excitement of
being able to start this new venture, he didn't seem to notice
the grief Stacy felt in leaving the baby. After all, he thought,
theirs was an equal marriage. He was enabling her to pursue
her career. Wasn't that what "new men" were supposed to do?
Wasn't this just another part of the partnership they had
promised each other in their wedding vows?

Stacy found herself resenting Samuel's new business and
then feeling guilty for that. He loved searching for books at
yard sales, attending book fairs, making new friends, all with
Rebecca in a baby backpack. So he was the one who saw
Rebecca's first smile, discovered her first tooth, watched her
take her first steps, took her to the park to play.

His bookstore business took most of their savings and did
little more than break even financially. As Stacy's salary was
needed to meet most of their financial obligations, she worked
longer and longer hours. She had less and less time with her
husband and her child. And she was coming home to a house
that was more and more cluttered and dirty.

They agreed that Samuel, with his flexible schedule, could
do most of the housework and laundry. But he just tossed

clothes into the washer and then into the dryer. If there were stains on Rebecca's clothes, that didn't bother him. Certainly not enough to trouble with prewashing or treating clothes with stain removers. Stacy was embarrassed by the stained clothes she often saw her daughter wearing.

When Stacy and Samuel discussed it, his solution was simple: if you want the clothes done differently, if that matters to you, you need to do the laundry.

When Stacy complained that so much clutter around the house made it difficult for her to relax when she got home, Samuel suggested that she needed to not be so fussy. Or if that mattered to her, perhaps she should do more picking up and cleaning.

One day Samuel brought home a box of old books for the store and set the box in the front hallway of the house. When Stacy arrived home, she noticed it. *If I complain*, she thought, *Samuel will just think I am being picky. I probably do need to relax my standards some.* And she ignored the box—every day—for three months.

Finally she exploded. When was he ever going to move that box of books out of the front hallway! Samuel was surprised.

"That's where those books are!" he said. "I thought I had lost them in some corner of the storeroom. I hadn't noticed them here. If they bothered you, why didn't you say something?"

In concluding her story, Stacy says:

"We started out with this equal division of responsibilities. But now it feels pretty unequal to me. The burden of housework and laundry falls mostly on me, because it matters to me. If I try to talk about it with Samuel, I either end up doing more work or feeling that I'm a picky nag. Either way I seem powerless to get him to do more housework. I don't think he even sees the dirty clothes on the bedroom floor, or the toys on the stairs. And I can't *not* see them.

"Samuel is content to let me bring in most of our money *and* do most of the housework. The long hours I've been working for the last few years have taken their toll on me. I'm so tired of my work, I'd give anything to take a break and stay home with Rebecca. She had her fourth birthday recently. Boy, that really hit me hard. In another year, she'll be in school. Oh, how I wish I could spend this last year at home with her!

"Samuel doesn't understand how I feel. He wonders why I don't appreciate the 'liberated man' I married. In those women's rights rallies, in all the 'working women' magazine articles, nobody told me how hard this would be. Now I feel that I lost the years when Rebecca was a baby."

New Rules to an Old Game

Recent generations have seen the establishment of a new social contract between husbands and wives. Old, traditional gender roles have been tossed out the window. Each couple has been freed to hammer out divisions of labor that work best for them.

At the outset of this revolution, many women envisioned a world in which both parents worked outside the home and both parents shared in the care of their children. "Women's lib" was supposed to liberate women as well as men from stifling roles.

So why do so many women feel anything but "liberated"?

We've already acknowledged that the sex roles portrayed on fifties-era television sitcoms were limiting in many ways. Those stereotypical roles were part of the problem, not a solution we should pursue now.

Some women *and* men felt forced into identities that didn't fit their talents or personalities. Many men, cut off from their homes, wanted to be more involved with their children than their own fathers had been. And many women wanted more in life than diapers and housework.

We certainly do not want to advocate a return to the roles caricatured on black-and-white television. And yet we've been surprised by the number of stressed-out women we've talked to who look back at life a generation or two ago and wish for the "simplicity" their mothers or grandmothers enjoyed.

Clear divisions of labor between husband and wife did have some advantages. At least the understood expectations of the past freed women from constant negotiations with the men they loved. Our mothers and grandmothers, in traditional situations, may not have enjoyed always being the one to wash the dishes. But at least they didn't quarrel with their mates over the issue. And they didn't get stuck doing the dishes *and* the yard work *and* the bills—with full-time employment on top of it all.

In addition, strictly defined roles empowered mothers to expect their husbands to provide for them financially when children were small. Such an arrangement allowed mothers of young children to focus on motherhood as their work. And the lower divorce rates and stricter divorce laws of the time enabled most mothers to feel secure in this arrangement.

Who Gets to Be "Man of the House"?

Recent societal changes have reduced the age-old pressure on men to be the primary provider. In our grandparents' generation, and sometimes even in our parents' generation, a man was expected to provide for his family. He lost status in the community if he did not. Only one or two generations ago, men were embarrassed if their wives had to work, even just to supplement their income.

And out of that attitude, many men of the fifties and sixties refused to "let" their wives develop their potential. That frustration was one of the roots of the women's liberation movement.

In contrast, many men today assume they have the right to expect their wives to work at jobs that make money. Society in general agrees. A man can even be considered liberated if, in supporting his wife's career, he pressures her to work. He experiences no corresponding societal pressure to respect his wife's desire to stay home and nurture their children. He can completely disregard his wife's conflicted mother-in-the-middle feelings *and* benefit financially. Society simply doesn't cultivate or reinforce in men an understanding of the significant role mothers play in the lives of their children.

In fact, we heard stories from women whose husbands were subject to ridicule and teasing at work for "letting their wives live off them." Mothers told us about judgmental in-laws raising serious questions with their husbands about such "unambitious," even "lazy," wives who stayed home with their children.

Woman after woman expressed to us their frustrations that full-time motherhood seemed to be the one option for which they received little support from their spouse. Mothers no longer have the power to expect the men in their lives to provide for them (either financially or emotionally) so that they can work at mothering small children.

Bait and Switch: Nobody Told Me the Price Would Be This High

Part of the problem with our new social contract between men and women is that most women enter that contract with little understanding of the intensity of the maternal feelings they will experience when they first hold that tiny baby in their arms. Only after a baby is born do many women fall in love with their new child. Only then do they discover that the myth of the superwoman does not fit their lives and their needs.

Some mothers, like Stacy, feel obligated to go through with a deal they struck without knowing the cost beforehand. Other mothers decide to stay home with their babies, and find their spouses resentful that they are no longer holding up their end of the original bargain.

Both groups include mothers who feel deceived by society, surprised and frustrated that no one told them the cost before they agreed to a major life decision, and angry about the contract they signed without understanding the fine print.

No Longer Members of the Same Team

Consider Emma and Fred, a married couple who had four sons and owned a Michigan farm in the early years of the twentieth century. Fred knew which work around the farm was his work: the plowing, the planting, the animals, the butchering, and the harvest. Emma knew which work belonged to her: the children, the chickens, the laundry, the gardening, the canning, the cooking, and the house. Although Fred and Emma adapted this in small ways to suit themselves, most of their work was prescribed by society. They spent little emotional energy negotiating roles. Their sons helped either Emma or Fred, depending on their ages and which work needed to be done during that season of the year.

Each day, day after day, Fred was able to see and appreciate the hard work Emma was doing. And Emma witnessed Fred's labor, too.

With shared commitment and effort, Emma and Fred bettered their family. They were a team, working together in complementary ways. And Emma's work in supervising and caring for their children clearly contributed to the fortunes of the family.

Looking back from our day, Fred and Emma seem almost as stereotyped as those comedy shows from the early days of television. But they were real enough. And many families of their times fit that general pattern. With variations, men and women throughout history have worked together in similar ways. Although there were exceptions, most families of Fred and Emma's times were members of the same team, working for the same goals.

Now let's compare them to a contemporary couple, Barbara and Ted.

Ted is an engineer. Barbara is a college instructor. They have two children, an eight-year-old son and a three-year-old daughter. Before their son was born, Barbara had planned to continue teaching. After the baby arrived, she changed her mind.

But in anticipation of starting a family, they had bought a house. The older their son grew, the more strongly Barbara felt about the need for her to stay home. The birth of their daughter doubled her resolve. But the longer Barbara stayed away from her job, the more pressure Ted felt about paying the mortgage out of one paycheck. Finally, at Ted's insistence, when their youngest was two, Barbara began teaching again, part-time.

As each college semester approaches, Ted brings up the possibility of Barbara teaching another course so she can bring in more money and get back onto the tenure track. With each semester, Barbara debates taking on one less course so that she can have more time with the children and do a better job with the house.

Like most couples of our times, Ted helps around the house more than his father ever did. But Barbara still does the great majority of the housework. With one preschooler at home and a school-age child involved in sports and other activities, Barbara has little time for even the routine cleaning and is constantly trying to get Ted to help more.

As Barbara negotiates for Ted to help more around the house, Ted negotiates for Barbara to help more financially. Both feel overwhelmed and overworked, and each wants the other to do more. They stand on either side of a divide, both often feeling alone.

Their individual goals are regularly in conflict, because they have differing expectations of each other's roles and differing sensitivities and concerns about the demands of their children. In lives where there are too many conflicting needs and too little time, many families have become adversarial. Like Barbara and Ted, many couples in our times no longer feel like a team, pulling together.

Instead, they play tug-of-war.

Our mother in the middle is not only torn between her children and her job. She also feels pulled between the needs of her husband and the needs of her children.

Mothers, like everyone else, long for support, encouragement, and affirmation for their work. But the one person to whom a women should be able to turn for those things, the father of her children, is often now the one who wants to pull her away from them. Which is at least part of the reason why many of the mothers to whom we spoke longed for the family teamwork enjoyed by the couples of Fred and Emma's time.

Your Money, My Money, Our Money

Cynthia works in customer service at Kmart. Rick is an automobile mechanic. They are the parents of two young sons. Their family lives in a rented double-wide trailer. After their first son was born, Cynthia returned to work right away. A year later Cynthia became pregnant again but suffered a miscarriage.

That was a turning point in Cynthia's life. "Until we lost the baby, I was intent on saving enough money for a down payment on a real house. But after the miscarriage, I decided that these were the only years I would have with our kids. A house could wait."

Cynthia dropped out of the workforce for four years. In that time, they had another baby boy. While at home, she scrimped and did without things; she and Rick continued to put a little into their savings account each month for the down payment.

When the baby was two, Rick took their savings to buy himself a motorcycle. He told Cynthia that it was his money—he could spend it on himself. Cynthia was angry, but she considered it his money, too. That's when Cynthia began working weekends at Kmart. "The hardest part of staying at home," Cynthia told us, "was not having any money of my own. That's mainly why I went back to working. I wanted to have some money, too."

Rick realizes that it's hard to be at home with two active boys. After all, he keeps the kids while she works on the weekends. But she produces nothing concrete for him to see.

So he doesn't view her mothering as "work." It doesn't bring a paycheck.

Cynthia knows that Rick "works." And she knows that he is working longer hours now, since she is home during the week. She seldom sees the results of his work: cars that have been fixed. But of course, he has a paycheck.

For too many mothers, the family game has changed from a team sport to individuals playing tug-of-war in all directions. And the only way some families keep score is with a paycheck.

Is It Work Only If I Get Paid?

Celeste worked in nursing until she had children. Then for twelve years she was an at-home mother. That time included stints as PTA officer, Brownie troop leader, Sunday school teacher, and a host of other volunteer positions that enriched the lives of her family and society in general.

But when her third and youngest daughter began school last year, she told a friend, "Allen [her husband] wants me to go back to work. He's had his eye on a new boat for a long time now. I guess I can't complain: he has let me stay home with the kids for twelve years. It's probably time for me to go back to work. It's just that I'm not really interested in nursing anymore."

Celeste feels a sense of indebtedness to her husband for postponing one of his dreams and "letting" her be an at-home mother. Neither she nor her husband seem to view the mothering of three children, and her constant involvement in volunteer service, as "work."

Many mothers spoke to us of a world they have fashioned around their motherhood. A world that meshes with the needs of their children. Work that is satisfying and enriching. The only trouble with this work is that it has psychic income but no financial paycheck.

We spoke to mothers who were PTA presidents, volunteered at schools and in hospitals, worked in food banks and homeless shelters, and served society in any number of other ways. Many women said they found fulfillment in such unpaid community service activities.

Some mothers even found creative ways to provide service and earn "a little money of their own" by doing things like baby-sitting for church functions or teaching aerobic classes for senior citizens. But not many women viewed such volunteer or part-time labor as *work*.

And neither did their husbands.

Don't Get No Respect

Like Margaret in chapter 1, a number of women who talked to us told about husbands who felt that they were "supporting me in my little hobby" if they stayed home with their children. Some husbands just didn't understand why their wives were tired or lonely after caring for preschool children all day. Other husbands of at-home moms just didn't understand why the house wasn't spotless when they got home.

Longing for Peace

Some leaders in the feminist movement believe that we are involved in a gender war (more on that in chapter 7). And we did indeed find mothers who felt at odds with the men in their lives, who get the good paychecks and do their pick of the housework.

But few of the mothers we talked to wanted to do battle with their husbands. They were tired of constantly negotiating with someone they loved. Mothers at home were tired of being pressured to "work," when they were already doing as much work as they could manage. Employed mothers were tired of coming home from a full-time job and finding themselves starting a second shift, where they also had primary responsibility for the kids and the house. Both groups of women were tired of knowing, with all their hearts, that caring for their children was important—and too seldom feeling that belief validated by their men.

As we will discuss in chapter 11, some women we talked with had found personal peace. They were the ones who usually received support from their husbands and considered that support essential.

Divorce: Losing the Ultimate Battle

Valerie took a day off work last year to accompany her son on a preschool field trip and picnic at a local park. As she sat with three at-home mothers and watched two-year-old Stephen squealing and laughing in delight as he raced across the playground with the other kids, Valerie's eyes began to well up with tears. "I've got to quit my job," she vowed to her friends. "I just can't keep missing out on this part of Stevie's life."

Yet today Valerie is still working and doesn't feel she can take the personal or professional risk of quitting—even for just a couple of years. Her marriage has been shaky since before Stephen was born. She feels that having her own career and income gives her at least a measure of security as she wonders and worries about an uncertain future.

Even without that immediate consideration, there's the professional issue. Taking even two or three years off from her career could put her at least that far behind her colleagues in the professional pecking order. She knows it would make it difficult, perhaps even impossible, to get back into her field if her husband left her and she needed to do so. There just aren't many careers in which "motherhood" is considered valuable, applicable experience with which to pad a résumé.

In our focus in this chapter on the "battle between the sexes," we need to acknowledge that not all mothers have a husband to do battle with. Single mothers in the middle face added challenges. And others, like Valerie, live in fear of losing the ultimate battle in their marriages.

Christine, a psychiatric social worker, and her first husband divorced when their children were two and three years old. Like most divorced women, she suffered a serious drop in her financial security. And several years passed before she remarried. Christine told us:

"One of the things I missed as a single parent was having someone to talk with about the cute things they did. No one else quite appreciates the cuteness. My mother did and I appreciate her for that.

"Since I've remarried, life has felt somewhat easier. Having a partner makes a huge difference, if for no other reason than just having someone to be at home with the kids when I have to work late. And to help with the endless taxiing that goes on. My husband gets the dinner when I work late. He talks with the children about their problems and in general helps to carry some of the workload.

"The bulk of it still rests with me—I am the woman and I am the natural parent. But it sure is nice to have some help.

"My husband also shoulders the primary responsibility for our financial well-being. It has been a tremendous relief to not be solely responsible for providing the family finances. I enjoy my career more when I'm not under that pressure. Having a partner makes it easier in terms of just having someone else to talk over the problems with—but yet, with him being a stepparent, his views are sometimes more objective than I want to hear.

"Over the past five years, my husband has begun to view the children as his own, and we share a real interest in them. Now he will tell stories about things they did when they were little and we'll laugh. Now we talk about what we need to do about this behavior or that report card. But for years, there was a lot of tension, blending a stepfamily—complicated by an anything-but-supportive ex-husband."

Divorced women like Christine experience a whole added meaning to the term mother in the middle.

One of the warning cries of feminism has been: "Each woman lives one divorce away from poverty." And research backs that up. From 1960 to 1993 the rate of divorce rose 140 percent.[1] In the year after a divorce, the woman suffers a drastic drop in her standard of living. The man experiences a gain.[2]

In her book *The Second Shift*, sociologist Arlie Hochschild writes:

> Divorce is an undoing of an economic arrangement between men and women. Reduced to its economic bare bones, traditional marriage has been what the economist Heidi Hartmann calls a "mechanism of redistribution": in a sense, men have "paid" women to rear their children and tend to their homes.[3]

But too many fathers—and mothers—no longer view rearing children and tending to a home as work. As a result, in too many households the paycheck belongs to the one who brings it home. And too many mothers live in fear of divorce and feel that they need to work to have a sense of security and "some money of their own."

In all the changes that have taken place in the relationships between men and women over the past few decades, some things have remained the same. Children still need mothers *and* fathers who are "crazy about them." And mothers still need support and encouragement in their care of children.

In all the talk about the mommy wars, it's easy to look at the ways in which society devalues mothers. But one of the most common problems we've found, a problem we've seen little research or commentary on, has been the number of women who have suffered from friendly fire on the home front. Too many mothers are feeling the least support and the most pressure from the very people they feel should most care for them. It's most hurtful, because it is so close and so personal and so disappointing to do battle with the men in their lives, the fathers of their children.

We live in an age when so many choices have opened up to women. Ironically, the one choice many women today tell us they don't have is to stay home with their children. Because that's the one option the men in their lives don't understand or support.

Six

Sister vs. Sister: An Uncivil War

*Women don't need men to criticize them, because we
beat each other up ... and we do a bang-up job.*

a mother of seven

Paula and her younger sister, Cindy, were about as close as
two girls could be while growing up. Paula was three years
old when Cindy was born. She remembers the first time their
mother let her hold the baby, how much she enjoyed helping
dress her. When Cindy was a preschooler, Paula was in grade
school. Paula would come home and play teacher to Cindy. By
the time Cindy started school, Paula had already taught her
the alphabet, numbers, and colors.

Growing up, Paula and Cindy shared a bedroom. Many
nights, they lay awake whispering in the dark, sharing secrets.
Anytime Cindy had questions or a problem, she usually went
to Paula. Paula was the big sister with all the answers, from
how to play games to what makeup to wear to which boys she
should date.

Paula went away to college, where she met Larry. They
married after graduation. Larry went to work as a teacher,
Paula as an accountant. When each of their two children were
born, Paula returned to her office after six weeks.

Cindy also went away for her first year of college. Then she decided to take a year or two away from school. Everyone, especially Paula, seemed to expect her to decide on a career. But what appealed most to Cindy was getting married and being a mother. She hadn't yet found any other "career" that seemed interesting to her. But she also hadn't found anyone she wanted to marry.

She spent a year as a short-term missionary in Honduras. Then Cindy returned and enrolled in college again. She met Tim in one of her classes, and less than a year later they were married.

For Cindy, it was a dream come true. She was in love with her husband. She and Tim had three daughters in nine years. Her homemaker lifestyle enabled her to volunteer her time at church, organizing a mother's-morning-out program. She became active in La Leche League and enjoyed being available to other young mothers who needed someone to talk to. She had time to take her children to the park and the library, to be the mother she had always wanted to be.

Cindy felt that her life was ideal except for one thing. Her older sister, Paula, continued to push Cindy to find a "career." Whenever they talked on the phone, whenever their families visited each other, Paula would suggest another career option for Cindy. She clipped out newspaper articles about job possibilities that she thought would work for Cindy.

Cindy told us sadly:

"Every time she says, 'You really ought to be doing something with your life!' I feel like screaming, 'But I am!' She just doesn't understand me. And she certainly doesn't think what I am doing is worthwhile. Sometimes I feel that we have nothing in common anymore. I would never want to force my sister to make the same choices I made. But it seems my choosing full-time motherhood is simply unacceptable to her."

Not only have many mothers been wounded by the friendly fire from the men in their lives but we often seem to be under attack from our own. Our own sisters. Other mothers. The very group who best ought to understand and empathize with the mother in the middle.

Women throughout history have been unified by such uniquely feminine and near-universal experiences as pregnancy, childbirth, nursing, and the nurturing and mothering of small children. In our grandmothers' day, women from almost any strata of society could gather and share with each other on any of these topics. Their stories would have been variations on the same theme. And they could have walked away from such a discussion with a feeling of support and a sense of belonging to the universal sisterhood of women. That same sense of sisterhood provided generations of women with emotional strength and a sense of purpose for their mothering.

Today that sisterhood has been fractured into as many factions as we have choices facing women. There are mothers, women who choose not to have children, and women who want children but are infertile (some of whom settle on adoption, while others pursue the newer route of science and technology). Then there are women who have natural childbirth, women who have medicated birth, and women who have cesarean sections. Some mothers breast-feed; others bottle-feed their babies.

While these motherhood choices are a natural part of our lives, they divide us into ever smaller and smaller groups of women who can truly empathize with each other. Divisions that limit our sources of support. One mother only half jokingly told us, "There are days when I want to join a support group of women like me: mothers of only children, who work part-time, had their baby at home, breast-fed them until they were toddlers, sent them to public school, are active in PTA, and . . ."

But of all the differing experiences dividing women today, the most emotional division—and what really triggered the mommy wars—is the differences between at-home mothers and employed women. Indeed, the gap is often so great between the groups that some mothers who work part-time told us they feel pressure and criticism from both sides. And whatever choices we make in our own lives, we find ourselves on opposite sides of this emotional division than someone we care deeply about—often painfully separated from our best friends, our own sisters, and sometimes even our own mothers.

Friend vs. Friend

A woman named Charlene told us:

"Carla and I were best friends when we worked in the office together. We ate lunch together most days and got together on weekends some. We never ran out of things to talk about!

"After Jack and I were married, Carla and I remained close friends. Then her son, Bradley, was born. When I heard her talking about her day care situation and how hard it was to leave her baby to come back to work—that's when I began asking myself, *When I have children, do I really want to continue working and face what Carla is facing now?*

"When our daughter, Angela, was born, I stayed out of work five months. And then when I did go back, I worked only part-time. But when our son, Andrew, was born two years later, I quit entirely.

"Carla and I still meet occasionally for lunch. But now we keep running out of things to talk about. And hardly a visit goes by without her asking, 'What do you do with your time?' and 'Isn't it boring to be home with two little kids?'

"All the mothers I know seem to be divided into two very distinct camps: those who work outside the home and those who don't. We don't dislike each other. We just don't have much in common."

Sister vs. Sister

Kitty is an at-home mother with one preschool daughter. She spoke poignantly of wanting more support from her extended family, of how she longed to know that they think she is a good mother. In another age, she might have discussed the joys and trials of motherhood with, and gained that longed-for support from, her sister-in-law, who not only lives nearby but also has a daughter the age of Kitty's little girl. But instead, Kitty feels she and her brother's wife are worlds apart. She told us:

"I remember one Saturday when her little girl was at our house playing with my daughter. I fed my niece some kiwi. So when her mother picked her up, I warned her that when she changed her daughter's diaper the next day, she'd see a bunch of kiwi seeds. 'Don't let it scare you,' I teased. My sister-in-law started laughing and said, 'I never see any of her diapers.'

"And I thought, *She never has to change a dirty diaper?* But then I realized that, in fact, she never really has to do any work with her daughter, because the day care people do it for her from 7:00 till 6:30 at night."

Since the primary focus of Kitty's life is taking care of her own little girl, it's no wonder Kitty feels as if she has little in common with her sister-in-law. They do live worlds apart.

Yet we also talked to women who felt that motherhood had strengthened and enriched their relationships with their sisters. Women who have, in sharing the little joys and daily trials of motherhood, opened new doors of intimacy with their female siblings and friends. But these testimonies only served to reinforce the point we're making here: the mothers who miss out on this deeper dimension of sisterhood have truly lost a satisfying source of support and encouragement.

Mother vs. Daughter

Rita planned to return to her job after her son was born. But when the baby came, she decided to try working part-time. Less than two months later she quit altogether. She says that's when she found herself at odds with her own mother:

"My mom always worked when we were small. She did not understand how I could want to work only part-time, much less quit altogether. We stayed at each other's throats the whole first year I took off. It began over breast-feeding. She would say, 'That baby's not getting enough milk. He's starving.' Of course, he was as fat as a pig, a roly-poly kid.

"But she *really* didn't understand why I didn't work, since my husband was having to hold down two jobs. When I got pregnant with my second child, she couldn't understand why we hadn't waited. And when I got pregnant the third time, she was completely baffled. Why would we want another baby? We already had a boy and a girl.

"Even now she's always asking what I am going to do about getting a job.

"I wish I had more support from my family. My mom knows I have hard or bad days with three small children. But her attitude is that I've made my own bed—now I need to lie in it. She just doesn't understand.

"Sometimes, when I'm ready to go crazy for adult company, I'll call to tell her I'm about to have lunch, and ask her over. She's retired now and only lives about five minutes away, but she'll say, 'I can't. I'm going to vacuum today.' And I think, *You've got all week to vacuum.*

"We disagree a lot."

Rita is not alone in feeling such conflict. We heard stories from women in both mommy-wars camps who found themselves at odds with their own mothers, separated by very different values and decisions.

On December 28, 1995, the *Wall Street Journal* ran a front-page article headlined "Some Adult Daughters of 'Supermoms' Plan to Take Another Path." As an introduction to several case studies of accomplished career women and their young adult daughters, the article observed:

> Determined to be great mothers, great wives, and great careerists at the same time, supermoms came of

age in the heady early days of the modern women's movement. To countless women, they were heroines. For some of their own daughters, however, being a supermom no longer seems like such a super idea.

This article quotes numerous twenty-something women who felt that their mothers worked too many hours at a job and too few as a mother. One commented, "I've always wished she could have been more of a mother." And yet another concluded, "I have trouble seeing how you can combine a fast-track career, marriage, and motherhood."

One daughter, who is being groomed to follow her mother as head of a company, said, "I'd be disappointed if the business didn't work out. But I would be more devastated if I neglected my family, because they are the ones who will always be there."[1]

Mothers spoke to us of the importance of having the approval, support, and empathy of their own mothers. Indeed, many women establish new and richer relationships with their own biological mothers, in the wake of experiencing motherhood for themselves. And because we (Charmaine and Deborah) know and appreciate how significant an influence our own moms have had in our personal lives as mothers, we are deeply saddened for those women who lose that unique mother-to-daughter support and miss out on such a powerful and empowering intergenerational connection.

Mothers vs. Other Women at Work

Janette is a nursing supervisor at a teaching hospital and a mother with two teenage children. Her first marriage, to her children's father, ended when her kids were preschoolers. She told us:

"As a single mother, some coworkers became very close friends, probably as a result of my being in such a very stressful situation, going through my divorce. Many of my colleagues either were, or had been, single mothers themselves and understood the difficulties I faced. Generally they seemed supportive of my parenting.

"However, as a salaried professional, I was expected to treat my job accordingly. I didn't leave work at a consistent time each day; I left work when there was a break in the action. I could not have kept that job long had I said, 'Gee, it's five o'clock and my kids expect me to pick them up now.' Or if I had left when I still had work that needed doing. The powers that be—even my boss, who was a mother herself—expected the job and career to be top priority. Their attitude was, *It's nice that you have kids, but you'd better be at that meeting tomorrow no matter what.*

"That has been true wherever I have worked. I learned early on never to call into work and say I had to stay home because one of my kids was sick. That would not be an excused absence—therefore no sick leave. So if my children were so sick that they couldn't go to school, it worked best for me to lie. I'd call in and say I was sick.

"Fortunately, I work in a field that is generally populated with people-oriented professionals who are perhaps more sensitive than most. I think that I have been fortunate and run into less of that [being forced to choose between job and children] than the average person.

"But business is business."

Many of the women involved in the feminist movement of the 1960s and 1970s envisioned a world of the future in which more women in the workplace meant a more caring, more empathetic business world. A working world in which women who succeeded would help younger women climb the corporate ladder behind them.

Instead, an increasing number of us now find ourselves in a world in which women, in order to compete in a man's work-world, have become afraid to rock the boat by asking for a more mother-friendly workplace. A surprising number of women seem unwilling to offer support for anything as unprofessional as motherhood. Many of the mothers we talked to have discovered that it's the other women at work, and often their female boss, who can be most resistant to accommodating motherhood at work.

———————————

Tina was an ambitious, up-and-coming professional woman for a child welfare advocacy group in Los Angeles. She had a very visible, responsible role, often speaking on behalf of her organization at seminars and to the press. Her successful performance of her job brought her glowingly positive job reviews and frequent pay raises. Tina had every reason to consider herself a valued member of her work team.

So when she became pregnant with her first child, she assumed that her organization would be very willing to provide a part-time work arrangement, a flexible work schedule that would allow her to maintain a part-time career and still fulfill her new responsibilities as a mother.

Tina was shocked, devastated, and more than a bit disillusioned by the response of her superiors, who instantly dismissed the idea—saying there was no way to do what she wanted. She would have to make a choice. She said:

"I felt so devalued by their decision! After several years of telling me how wonderful and talented I was, they were willing to just toss me out. The skills I brought to the organization weren't considered valuable enough for them to make room for my motherhood. Part of what made it so difficult for me was that the person who took the strongest stance against allowing me to work part-time was a woman. A mother whose own children were already in school."

For her book *Prisoners of Men's Dreams*, Suzanne Gordon interviewed women who were doctors, lawyers, academics, scientists, and businesspersons and concluded:

All are torn between intense pressure to compete on men's terms and the deep need to be nurtured and nurture in a rich world of relationships. The women want to attain mastery and recognition in their fields. But because this means being treated as an equal to a man in a man's world, they are forced to sacrifice their commitment to their own caring goals—the desire to treat colleagues or subordinates well and nurture their development, empower others, maintain social relationships, and preserve a balance between work and love, and work and family life.[2]

Hope learned this truth the hard way. She was a department head at a major denominational church's national office for eight years. She had planned to return to her job after the birth of her first baby. She told us:

"I loved my work. I had just reached the point that I had been striving for. The month before my son was born, I won a national award for my work.

"I had considered leaving my work to be with the baby, but I wasn't sure I could. I was making more money at my job than my husband was at his. But I decided about thirty minutes after he was born that I wasn't going back.

"My boss was also my best friend: she was in my wedding; she was my mentor. She was only a couple of years older than me. We were really close. She had a baby just a year before my son was born.

"When I went in and told her I was going to quit to stay home, she flipped out. It was very painful. She said some really ugly things. She told me that I was letting all women down. She made me feel as if I were destroying everything every woman had ever fought for as far as freedom of choice. She told me that I was making all the sacrifices and my husband wasn't making any. And what would we do if he lost his job?

Couldn't my husband quit instead? It hurt me deeply that she couldn't accept my decision.

"She was my best friend and our friendship ended suddenly and completely—even to this day. I recently went into the office to see everybody, and she was very cold. That still hurts.

"In our office, there were several older women, mothers whose kids were grown. They would catch me in the elevator when it was just me and them and would whisper, 'You're not going to regret this.' And 'This is a good thing you're doing.' They were real supportive, but why couldn't they say it out loud? It was the most bizarre thing that they didn't think they could say that out loud."

Other mothers experience their greatest conflicts in the workplace with younger career women, ambitious women who have been told that they can have it all. Suzanne Gordon calls them the "No Cares Cohort."[3] With neither children nor older parents to care for, they often resent and resist any accommodations made for other women colleagues in either circumstance.

Martha took four months off from work at an insurance office when her daughter was born. "Our district manager was in her thirties and did not want children," Martha told us. "Her career was more important. Everyone knew that's how she felt." She said that most of the mothers at her company felt the impact of the district manager's attitude and responded by working long hours and taking short maternity leaves.

We heard numerous stories from mothers who felt they'd been ambushed by other women in the workforce. Some mothers who said they'd been able to establish close friendships on the jobs told us that those friendships rarely extended to motherhood-work conflicts. All in all, the mothers we talked to said that after three decades of feminism and all the corresponding advances in women's rights, their business world did not yet, in any significant way, resemble a mother-and-child-friendly place.

Divided and Deceived

The deep divisions separating so many women today from friends, from sisters, from their own mothers, and from other women with whom they routinely interact in the "community" (or workplace) have left many modern mothers to lead very isolated, emotionally impoverished personal lives. With traditional support systems of family, friends, and neighbors now removed, and with the corresponding loss of age-old sources of societal "wisdom," there just aren't many places for women today to turn for encouragement, practical knowledge, or how-to advice for dealing with the common challenges and problems of everyday life.

So we increasingly look to the media—a more impersonal yet pervasive source for everyday help and how-to information. We turn to magazines instead of Mom or Grandma for everything from recipes to toilet-training tips. And more frightening yet, we use talk shows rather than our next-door neighbors' example as our gauge of societal standards and practices on everything from child discipline to sex education.

Even those mothers today who've been able to maintain a more traditional support system read popular women's magazines, watch the same television networks, and absorb the media messages about motherhood.

And not only do many of those media messages undermine mothers and devalue motherhood but many of them are downright deceitful, dishonest, and demeaning to the very women they purport to serve.

An entire book could be written on this subject. Our comments here will have to be limited mostly to the role played by women's magazines in regard to the topic of our book and their treatment of relevant issues concerning mothers and work.

In chapter 4 we sampled from the plethora of pertinent data available from research and studies on mother-child attachment. It's hard not to see a conspiracy of silence among women's magazines which have almost ignored those findings.

Just as appalling is the reluctance of the media in general, and women's magazines in particular, to inform mothers of the health concerns that the medical research community is raising about the mushrooming day care industry (more on that in chapter 10).

However, it's not just what women's magazines don't tell mothers that causes us concern. It's the misleading and some-times blatantly dishonest things passed off as truth and wis-dom—information offered as practical help and guidance for readers desperate for wisdom in making the toughest, most heart-wrenching decisions of their lives as women and mothers.

Just one telling example: In the early 1980s, a number of magazines carried articles reporting on studies that showed that "working mothers spend almost as much time caring for their children as nonworking mothers." Employed mothers who might be feeling guilty about leaving their children in order to work no doubt found comfort in this report.

Conversely, the average at-home mother found little encouragement. And any mothers whose husbands were already pressuring them to go back to work lost some ammu-nition for their battle to stay home.

But can that "fact," so widely reported by women's maga-zines, actually be the case? The original source of this so-called fact was a publication entitled *Families That Work: Children in a Changing World*, put out in 1982 by the National Research Council. In the chapter entitled "The Influence of Parent's Work on Children's School Achievement," the report indeed stated, "Studies of time use suggest that working mothers spend almost as much time caring for their children as do nonworking mothers." According to the studies, on which this original article was based, at-home mothers spent only six and a half hours a week—less than an hour a day—more taking care of their children than working mothers did.

But a closer look at this research reveals at least two glaring flaws in the report. The first problem was what the time-use experts had counted as time spent "caring for children." The mothers in this study could count time as "care for children" only if they were taking care of children and not doing anything else. Any real-life activities—talking with a child while grocery shopping, listening while fixing supper, doing the laundry together—did not count as time spent in "caring for children."

The second problem was the highlighted conclusion—that working mothers spent "almost as much" time in "child care" as at-home moms. The real "fact" that came to light was that even with such a narrow definition of child care, at-home mothers still spent almost one more hour each day caring for their children.[4]

So how fair was this study and the reports on it? Is conversation with a child while folding clothes an insignificant way to care for a child? Is there no value in time spent with a child while walking a dog? And what about time spent driving places together in the car? Most mothers count such informal moments with their children to be some of the sweetest minutes of the day.

But what this research and all the magazines that rushed to report on it were really telling mothers was that the only "mothering" that counts is exclusive, focused time, like reading books, changing diapers, and actually playing games with the kids. Anything else they do as mothers, any other time they spend including children in their own daily activities, is meaningless.

What could be more demeaning?

Were the readers of the magazines told about the holes in this report? No. How many mothers actually had the time to dig out the original to judge for themselves? Very few.

The magazines sold copies with their misleading headlines. And they probably comforted a number of women feeling guilty about their jobs. But they also did a disservice to employed moms—to the extent that they convinced women to accept such a narrow definition of mothering and think that none of the little things mothers have always done to interact with their children and include them in the course of daily activities even counts as real mothering.

But even beyond what the magazines don't report and the intentionally misleading articles they sometimes do print, there's yet another anti-motherhood media message that shines through loud and clear.

It's a matter of image. And as Madison Avenue tell us so often and so loudly that much of society has come to believe it, "Image is everything!"

Ironically, Betty Friedan herself blasted women's magazines for their culpability in furthering the feminine mystique. She accused the print media of stifling women with stereotypical, fluff journalism that only served to glamorize housework and traditional women's roles such as nurse, teacher, mother, and housewife.[5]

By the late seventies and early eighties, the pendulum had swung almost 180 degrees. As Suzanne Gordon observed:

> The new feminine heroine was a tailored Charlie's Angel who carried an attaché case rather than a .38 and who could "role model" for a new breed of sisters who wanted to "network"—that is, to cut deals, make killings, and get to the top of the corporate heap.[6]

While you still find many articles about women who somehow fit mothering into their careers, how often do you see the story written the other way around? What gets glamorized today in women's magazines? Certainly not motherhood.

Indeed, the media, having usurped the more personal, traditional role of family, friends, and neighbors as the source of societal norms and collective wisdom, often seems to lead the attack on motherhood today, firing some of the most damaging salvos in the mommy wars. But the media is hardly the only— or the first—element of society to demean and devalue motherhood today.

We'll examine some other assaults on motherhood in the next chapter.

A Great Divide

But here, as we wrap up our discussion of sister vs. sister, it's with a true sense of sadness that we have to acknowledge and accept this truth: women who were once unified by the universal experiences of motherhood now find themselves divided into sometimes bitter and contentious camps. Those on either side find it difficult to defend their personal choices without being—or at least seeming to be—critical of friends or sisters who have made the other decision.

Most of us believe that the motherhood choices we make will have long-lasting effects on our children and our families. We want desperately to make the wisest decisions. But only time—years of it—will tell if we will look back with regret.

We all want so badly to be "right." And that makes it hard for us not to look at other mothers as "wrong" when they have made decisions so different from our own. So it is that many of those conflicting decisions become skirmishes in the mommy wars.

Sometimes the mother on the other side of the battle lines is a sister, a mother, or a longtime friend, the very women to whom we would normally turn to for support, encouragement, and affirmation. That can leave us feeling wounded . . . alone . . . defensive . . . insecure.

That's the bitter pain so many of us feel when we're pitted against our own—sister vs. sister.

Seven

Children Caught
in the Cross Fire

*Babies in whom no one takes a deep and continuing
interest may forfeit the promise of birth.*

Charles Leroux and Cindy Schreuder,
the *Chicago Tribune*[1]

More than twenty years ago now, I (Deborah) landed my first job out of college, working at an upscale, expensive day-care center in a small city. Part of what attracted parents to this day care center—part of what had prompted me to apply there—was the facility. It was in a large, beautiful old Victorian house, very quaint, very homey. The director and her husband lived upstairs, with the downstairs devoted to the day care.

The director seemed such a nice person, always very professionally dressed. She gave an impressive tour, talking about the "developmental objectives" and the "creative curriculum" of her day-care center. In the front hallway, she kept a bulletin board with attractively arranged pictures of children from the center, engaged in activities and on field trips.

I was the teacher of twenty-eight three-year-olds in a room licensed for eighteen children. I had an assistant teacher for the first half of the day, until naptime. For the remainder of the afternoon, I was on my own.

But even in the mornings, the director often pulled my assistant out of my room to do other things. She filled in for absent teachers or when someone quit abruptly—something that happened often. When the cook called in sick, my assistant went to the kitchen for the day. On many days, I was by myself with twenty-eight children from 8:00 in the morning until 4:00 in the afternoon.

My assistant teacher quit the day the director pulled her out of my class to help paint the outside of the day care center. She had lasted about a month—longer than any of the other assistant teachers subsequently hired to help me.

My mornings were spent simply trying to maintain minimal control of twenty-eight three-year-olds, all desperate for some individual attention from an adult. I was expected to do an art or craft activity with the children each day, something cute or impressive for them to take home to their parents. That usually took all morning to accomplish.

After naptime, I would take all the children out on the playground, where I would sit on a bench and pull a child onto my lap and talk to him or her. I set up a written schedule: six children each day, one at a time, on a rotating basis. I knew it wasn't much, but that was the only way I could be sure that each child got my individual attention at least once a week.

Most of the parents of the children in my room were professionals. They would arrive in nice cars, wearing business suits. This was the most prestigious and pricey place in town to send a child. I overheard parents talking about how this center was expensive but it was worth it to get quality care for their children. I wanted to shake those parents! And suggest that they stop and count the number of children in my room. Couldn't they see how crowded we were? Why didn't one of them, just once, ask me a direct question about what was going on in the classroom?

By the time of the school's annual fall trip to a local pumpkin farm, I was beginning to realize that class size wasn't the only example of appearances being deceptive. The director actually collected money for field trips from all the children, then selected only two children, one boy and one girl, from each class to go on the outing. If the parents asked their children about the field trip and got blank looks, the parents simply assumed the people at the day-care center were telling the truth. After all, on the bulletin board were photos of children from every class at the pumpkin farm. And since we had read a book about a pumpkin farm, some of the children talked about that, and the parents assumed they were talking about an actual trip.

As I learned more and more about the problems of the center, I made dozens of phone calls—to the Better Business Bureau and to the Department of Family and Children Services (DFACS). Finally, only a week after the pumpkin farm field trip, DFACS showed up for an inspection, apparently in response to my calls. But their policy was to phone in advance. So the director knew the day ahead of time. She had the place shining. And thirty minutes before the DFACS inspector arrived, half my class was loaded into one of the school vans for an aimless drive around town until the director turned on the back porch light. That was her signal that it was OK for them to return. So while DFACS inspected, I had a comfortable fifteen children in my care, with an assistant teacher. The inspector was in and out of my room in three or four minutes, without bothering to ask me a single question.

The next week, I resigned. After three months, that day-care center had only one other teacher who had stayed there longer than I had. Yet part of me wanted to stay. I wondered, *Who else would take care of my children? Surely it was better for the students to have me, to whom they were attached, even under horrible circumstances.*

But morally I decided I couldn't stay. I felt as if I were lying to the parents by not telling them that there had been no field trip for their children. By not talking to them about the deplorable conditions. And as much as I loved those children and wanted to teach them, I knew I was not meeting their needs.

I have spent more than two decades in the field of early childhood education since I left that day-care center. During that time, I have directed, taught in, observed, and evaluated a wide variety of other day-care programs. None have looked as bad as that first center where I worked. However, I remind myself, even that day care looked good to the people who didn't work there every day.

Many day-care centers, like the one I later directed, did everything to meet National Association for the Education of Young Children (NAEYC) standards. But I have rarely seen a day-care center where children got enough adult attention. Or where children had their needs fully met. Even in good day care situations, children are often competing for the attention and affection of the adults there.

The Child in the Middle

While this book is addressed to, and focuses on, the *mother* in the middle of the mommy wars, while we identify with the women who have shared their stories with us, we're also deeply concerned for the children of our day and of generations to come. What is often forgotten in the midst of the powerful emotions expressed by mothers in the middle, what we all need to acknowledge, is that our children are also caught in the cross fire. The same world that pulls mothers in too many different directions often ignores the needs of our children.

Psychologist Urie Bronfenbrenner writes:

> In a world in which both parents usually have to work, often at considerable distance from home, every family member, through the waking hours from morning till night, is "on the run." The need to coordinate conflicting demands of job and child care, often involving varied arrangements that shift from day to day, can produce a situation in which everyone has to

be transported several times a day in different directions, usually at the same time—a state of affairs that prompted a foreign colleague to comment: "It seems to me that in your country, most children are being brought up in moving vehicles."[2]

That observation may be more accurate than most of us would like to admit. Many of our children are being brought up in group care situations, with a procession of different adults supervising their care. And the time in which their parents meet their needs for love and attachment is squeezed into a few "quality" moments here and there. Often that "quality" time is in the car, between commitments, while the parent battles traffic and the child fights for fleeting moments of attention or affection.

The Value of a Child

We live in an age when the government periodically calculates and publishes updated tallies of projected expenses for raising a child. The figures are always staggering. Couples routinely talk about "waiting until we can *afford* a baby." When we encounter someone with three or more children, we wonder how they will be able to provide financially for such a large family.

We are a generation of women practiced at controlling our reproductive destinies. Even birth control may well have played a subtle role in the devaluing of children. Children are now a choice, something that can wait until we have our careers established, our finances in order. Pregnancy can be prioritized on our list of life goals. And this attitude, carried to its extreme, tells us that when a pregnancy is inconvenient, we can have an abortion. After all, it is only a fetus. (And that's the ultimate devaluing of both motherhood and children.)

In this day and age when we as women listen to our biological clocks ticking at the same time that we are asking ourselves if we are ready to be "tied down" with a baby, sometimes we forget the transcendent value of children—their intrinsic worth. We have lost sight of the rich texture that children bring into our lives. And in our choices, we often forget to weigh the eternal significance of our children.

What Do Children Need?

It's only this context, this recognition of a child's inherent value, that gives meaning to the sacrifices required to meet the needs of children. For modern American society too often pits the needs of children against the needs of their parents—particularly their mothers.

The truth is—and always has been—that the needs of children and their mothers are inextricably intertwined. Because one of the driving motivational needs of most mothers is to rest assured that their children's needs are met. Indeed, that's one of the greatest sources of tension we hear in the passionate voices of mothers in the middle: this tug-of-war between mothers' needs and those of their children is an internal one. Which says to us we will never successfully meet the needs of mothers without first—or at least simultaneously—addressing the needs of their children.

A Minicourse in Child Development 101

So what do child development experts tell us our children need in order to learn and develop their potential?

We talked in chapter 4 about the important role mothers play in their *infants* learning trust. That when a baby cries, she is telling us that she needs something—food, a dry diaper, warmth, comfort. When someone picks her up in response to those cries, she develops a sense of trust and power. *When I cry, someone responds. The world must be an OK place.*

We know that infants need to form a strong attachment to at least one person: a familiar, loving person who learns to read that baby's signals and with whom the baby develops an intricate, mutually interactive, mutually rewarding relationship. This initial relationship, this "essential partnership," is the foundation for a child's interaction with others for the rest of his life. Children who fail to develop a sense of trust or who do not establish that necessary attachment may struggle with issues of trust and intimacy for the rest of their lives.

We all know jokes or perhaps have our own stories to tell about *two-year-olds* and the way they always say, "No!" As frustrating as that stage can be, saying no is an essential developmental milestone, for all toddlers are wrestling with independence and autonomy. They are discovering that they have the power to say no. Saying no when mother is saying yes is one way a toddler has of achieving separation and independence.

Second only to "no" in a two-year-old vocabulary must come "Me do it myself!" Toddlers need to learn how to do things for themselves—a process resulting in much frustration and eventually some success. They need a patient, loving person who offers them choices and opportunities to try new things—where they often fail but also sometimes succeed in their efforts. This loving adult must understand the child well enough to gauge his level of frustration—knowing when that frustration will motivate the child to try again, until he achieves success. At other times, the adult may intervene and help the child just enough. That's a delicate balance. The best and most sensitive of mothers achieve that balance only some of the time.

Children whose efforts to attain independence are often thwarted, who are not allowed or encouraged to "do it themselves," or who meet with too much frustration will develop a sense of shame, a feeling of incompetence.

Three-, four-, and five-year-olds have a drive for exploring, trying out the world, both in motor skills and language skills. Erikson called it "initiative."[3] Children this age ask questions endlessly, as a part of their language exploration and also their exploration of the world. Any mother who's been through this stage will no doubt remember when her child spewed questions like an auctioneer on amphetamines. Just listening to that endless stream of Who? What? Where? When? How? and Why? questions is exhausting. Especially when you know that any answer you give would trigger another barrage of queries.

Now imagine a roomful of four-year-olds, fifteen or twenty active minds, capable of burying their teacher at any given moment with an avalanche of questions. You may begin to rethink the pay scale at the average day-care center.

Twenty-year day-care veteran Dorothy Conniff pinpoints the concern this way:

> Learning to pose questions and receive information that is satisfying is a key social as well as intellectual experience in a child's development. Children who don't have a successful experience at this stage or whose experience is frustrated or perverted stop participating in the learning process. They stop expressing their questions and eventually may stop thinking them up.... And this is the most consistent drawback of day-care centers where staff are overloaded and inexperienced.[4]

This is also the age at which imagination takes flight. Dolls and toys are used to act out imaginary scenarios. Play is the way in which children learn. Children need a lot of acceptable choices and much undirected play time in which to explore at their own pace and in their own way. Sadly, too many group care situations are highly structured in order to maintain discipline and order.

Five- to seven-year-olds have shifted developmental gears. They have become ready for more formal teaching, ready to begin learning the skills necessary for success as an adult.

Some of the mothers who shared with us found that as their children grew older, work became easier to mesh with their motherhood responsibilities. But school-age and teenage children still need their mothers. Our relationships with our children evolve, slowly and unevenly, toward an adult-to-adult interaction. So children never outgrow their need for someone who believes that they are special, who knows them and still loves them unconditionally, someone who is crazy about them.

Jody, a mother of three, is a graphic designer who worked full-time, then part-time when her children were younger. But when her oldest started school, she found it harder and harder to combine her job with the care of her children, until after much soul searching, she resigned.

"The older my children were, the harder it became for me," Jody told us. "Particularly when they got into school. The children needed more than a baby-sitter. They needed parenting in a variety of instances: help with homework and more than driving to all their various activities. They needed parenting in situations with their friends, someone to talk to about what was going on in their lives. But when I had crazy deadlines, I could hardly take time to say hello to my children, much less *do* anything with them. I finally decided that my priority was our life and our children."

Jody still takes on occasional freelance work but has become comfortable with her new life. "It works for my family, and hence for me," she concluded.

Too many of the children of this generation are growing up hungry. Not hungry for food but hungry for someone to trust, hungry for success in doing things for themselves, hungry for answers to their questions. They come home to empty houses where no one asks them about their day. They sit in swings with no one to push them, calling out to the world, *"Look at me!"*

How are we trying to meet their needs?

We spend more and more money on day care.

The government subsidy of the child care market has increased from $8 million in 1965 to $7 billion in 1990. Consumer expenditures for child care have increased over that same time frame from $4.6 billion to $20.5 billion.[5]

Which begs the question . . .

Where Have All the Good Day-Care Centers Gone?

A 1995 newspaper headline over a nationally distributed wire service article stated, "Day Care Often Dismal, Study Concludes." The subheading went on, "Just One in Seven Centers Considered Good."

That newspaper article surprised us. Not that only one in seven day care centers would be considered "good." After all, with our experience and research for this book, we knew how serious the day-care crisis had become. No, what seemed surprising was that the mainstream press was talking about the real issues in day care.

The study itself was titled "Cost, Quality, and Child Outcomes in Child Care Centers" and was conducted by researchers at the University of Colorado at Denver, UCLA, the University of North Carolina, and Yale.[6]

These researchers concluded, "The level of quality at most U.S. child care centers, especially in infant-toddler rooms, does not meet children's needs for health, safety, warm relationships, and learning." The study also found that most child care is "sufficiently poor to interfere with children's emotional and intellectual development."

This was hardly news to anyone in the field of early childhood education. In 1987 a publication by the National Association for the Education of Young Children expressed this concern:

> Developing secure attachment relationships is among the most important developmental tasks for young children. Evidence is clear that children in child care do not replace their attachment to their parents with attachment to their child care provider. At the same time, however, children do get attached to their caregivers and use them as a secure base during the

day.... The loss of an attachment figure can be very painful to a young child. When these observations are juxtaposed with the 40 percent annual turnover among center-based child care providers and 60 percent turnover among home-based providers, *there is tremendous cause for concern.*[7] (Emphasis ours.)

How's a Parent to Know?

In the April 25, 1995, issue of *Woman's Day* magazine, writer Beth Levine talked about the challenge of finding acceptable day care for her son:

> Day care in America is such a hodgepodge, antiquated affair that parents are forced to take a leap of faith with the well-being of their child that they wouldn't take with any other part of their lives.... These people are strangers. You wouldn't give them the keys to your house.... You wouldn't tell them your cash card number. And yet you are supposed to hand them your child and feel OK about it?[8]

In the University of Colorado study, parents greatly overestimated the quality of the care their child was receiving. Even at centers that were rated poor to mediocre by the study observers, 90 percent of the parents rated their child's day care as "very good."

Like the parents at the day-care center where Deborah worked twenty years ago, most parents today don't often ask the right (or hard) questions. Perhaps it's because they don't know what they will do about child care if the answers aren't what they want them to be. Having taken a "leap of faith" with the welfare of their children, many parents seem reluctant to have that faith disillusioned.

Often mothers who use day care feel that they have no other choice. So knowing that the center they have chosen is less than what they wanted, many of them believe what society keeps telling them: that children are flexible; that other children have survived day care, so their child will, too; that day care will make their child more independent, more socially advanced. In other words, they are buying into the not-so-subtle message that "children don't really need their mothers."

So Many Children, So Few Day Care Slots

Complicating the child care crisis is the fact that in many areas of the country, the demand for day care far exceeds the number of day care slots available. Many parents settle for what day care they can find, however inadequate, and hope for the best. But underneath it all, most mothers who use day care wonder what happens during the day when they are not there. And most feel caught in the middle between job, day care, the needs of their children, and the financial needs of their families.

So Many Children, So Few Adults

Another issue in day care is the adult-to-child ratio. The National Association for the Education of Young Children (NAEYC) has set standards for this. Their recommendations: one adult for every three to four infants, one adult for every four to five two-year-olds, and one adult for every eight to ten three- and four-year-olds.[9]

One adult to four babies? Consider that one-to-four scenario for a few moments. Dorothy Conniff, who has worked in the day care field for twenty years, considered the challenge and began to add up the time figures. She figured each baby would need:

- Feeding: twenty minutes every three hours or so
- Diapering: ten minutes every two hours or so
- Cleanup: two minutes or so for hand washing and cleanup between each diaper change

Conniff pointed out that from a baby's perspective, that doesn't add up to too much care.

But consider the person caring for four babies. In a typical eight-and-a-half-hour day, that adds up to sixteen diaper changes—two hours and forty minutes of changing diapers. The person would spend four hours feeding babies, a total of twelve feedings. It would take forty minutes of the day just to clean up and wash your hands. That adds up to seven hours and twenty minutes spent on the simple physical necessities of the babies. And that's if the babies stay on schedule.

Conniff's conclusion?

> Since feeding and diaper changing are necessarily one-on-one activities, each infant is bound to be largely unattended during the five-plus hours that the other three babies are being attended to. So if there's to be any stimulation at all for the child, the caregiver had better chat and play up a storm while she's feeding and changing. . . . Obviously, such a schedule is not realistic. In group infant care based on even this four-to-one ratio, babies will not be changed every two hours, and they will probably not be held while they're fed.[10]

So Many Children, So Many Different Caregivers

Marlene was a cashier at a small bank when her daughter, Callie, was born. Reluctant to give up her excellent benefits, not to mention a job she really loved, Marlene went back to work six weeks after Callie's birth. For the next year, she had her daughter in a day care center with the best reputation in town. "But they went through staff so fast, there was no sense of stability," she complained. "I felt guilty leaving her every day without feeling sure what kind of care she was receiving." She finally gave up her job, because she just couldn't find a day care situation she felt good about.

High staff turnover is considered by many child development experts to be the most serious problem in day care today.

We have already talked about the importance of a significant adult for a baby to become attached to. Such an attachment is essential for the development of a sense of security and trust.

Children in day care form an attachment to parents at home and also to the teacher at school. Indeed, while we often call day care workers "teachers," they are more accurately termed "mother substitutes."

Children need consistent caregivers, a familiar face, someone with whom to form an attachment. But when a child becomes attached to a teacher and that teacher leaves, the child experiences loss and grief. Many children in day care experience that loss on a regular basis.

According to the most recent National Child Care Staffing Study, done in 1992 by the Child Care Employee Project, teachers in child care centers leave their jobs at a rate of 26 percent each year. That is three times the average annual turnover rate of all U.S. companies.[11] (Other findings, including the NAEYC report cited earlier, suggest even higher turnover rates.) Such staff turnover is a reliable indicator of poor-quality day care.

According to the University of Colorado research, one of the characteristics of a "good quality" day care was a center in which "children enjoyed close relationships with adults, and teachers focused on the individual needs of the children." Six out of every seven centers studied did not meet this standard.

In another study, infants and toddlers who experienced more teacher turnover were "less likely to engage in competent play with peers and objects.... Moreover, in a study of first-grade students' school adjustment, the stability of prior child care arrangements predicted academic progress."[12]

Why do day care teachers leave so often?

Low pay is part of the answer. Teachers in day care centers often work at little more than minimum wage. Child care workers are in the lowest 10 percent of all wage earners.[13]

Low prestige is another turnover factor. Consider, for example, the U.S. Department of Labor's list of skill ratings of various jobs. The lowest skill ranking of all jobs listed is 887 (the higher the number, the lower the rating). A dog trainer is ranked 228. A nursery school teacher is 878.[14] The message is clear: it doesn't take much to be a mother substitute.

Yet another reason for the high turnover in day care workers is the difficult working conditions found in most of the industry. People in child care usually have chosen this field because they enjoy working with children. Such people rarely find fulfillment in day care centers where there are too many children and too little time to meet the needs of those children. So teacher frustration and burnout are high.

The end result is that too many of the children in too many day care centers experience a constantly changing procession of important adults in their lives. What we as adults term "teacher turnover," children experience as personal *loss*.

But that's only one of the problems with day care today. We'll examine more in the next chapter.

Eight

More Children Caught in the Cross Fire

If all that children receive is custodial care and morally careless education, their bodies will mature but their souls will not. If the moral representatives of society do not reach children, television and the streets will.

Amitai Etzioni[1]

Jenny returned to her job as an accountant when her daughter, Jordan, was three months old. Less than two weeks later, Jordan woke up in the night with her first ear infection. After ten days of antibiotics, the ear infection recurred. Another ten days of medicine was followed by only two weeks of health. The next three months had two more episodes of otitis media, each requiring twenty days of antibiotics. Jenny told us:

"When Jordan was six months old, I got a call from the day care center. She was running a fever and pulling on her ear. When we finally got home that day, I sat down and cried. I had returned to work because we needed my income. But it seemed most of my income was going to pay doctor bills.

"Then I stopped crying and picked up a pencil and a pad of paper. On one side of the paper, I listed my earnings. On the other, I listed my work-related expenses: the cost of day care;

Jordan's medical bills; the cost of her antibiotics. Then I began to think of the other expenses I hadn't considered before: how often we now ate supper out; the cost of the convenience foods I had begun to buy when I went back to work.

"We had been talking about hiring someone to do house-work once a week. So I added that cost onto the bottom of my expense sheet.

"When I totaled the figures, I found I was working for less than twenty dollars a week, roughly eighty dollars a month. I decided that afternoon that we couldn't afford for me to work."

So Many Children, So Many Germs

While child development experts worry about attachment issues in regard to day care, members of the medical community often consider the health effects to be the most serious drawback to group care of children.

Children in day care settings are two to four times more likely to contract infectious disease, as compared to preschool-aged children reared at home. Otitis media—the ear infections Jordan suffered—and upper respiratory illnesses are among the most common problems.[2]

In an article in *Patient Care* entitled "Day Care Infections: Children at Risk," the authors stated:

> During the first thirty-six months of life ... children in day care centers had significantly more infections during each year than children in home care. ... Moreover, children in day care had significantly more severe illnesses than children in home care. ... Rates of infection, duration of illness, and the risk of hospitalization all tended to stabilize or decrease in children by their third year in day care.[3]

Disease in day care poses the most serious risks to the youngest children. Babies have more immature immune systems and are therefore more vulnerable to infections. Children who begin day care at the age of three to four are better ready for the exposure to the variety of infectious organisms found in most day care settings.

According to the authors of an article in the *Journal of the American Medical Association*, four factors contribute to the transmission of infectious diseases in child day care:

1. Large numbers of children are in close physical contact.
2. Infants and toddlers have poor personal hygiene.
3. Young children are susceptible to a variety of infectious organisms.
4. Infected children may be highly contagious before the onset of symptoms, and some infected children remain asymptomatic.[4]

And of course, day care workers vary greatly in their use of good hygiene.

Who's Telling Mothers the Truth?

Knowing, from Deborah's experience in the field, that there continue to be numerous health-related issues facing the day care industry, we decided to research the latest concerns for this book. First stop was a local public library, starting with a computer search for the current information on day care. We found not one single article on "health and day care," either positive or negative. Looking into the *Readers' Guide for Periodical Literature* proved just as fruitless. (We did find articles on day care and child abuse, a serious but much less prevalent problem.)

Next stop was a medical school library at a major university hospital. A single computer query on "day care and health aspects" turned up no less than 117 articles in current (within the past five years) mainstream medical publications. We were familiar with some of the issues discussed: for example, the role that day care plays in accelerating the evolution of antibiotic-resistant bacteria, those new strains of "superbugs" that researchers at the Centers for Disease Control are beginning to worry about. But other topics covered were new to us: for example, we didn't know that the air quality in day care centers is a source of concern. In one Canadian study, 90 percent of the centers tested failed to meet the government's minimum air-quality standards for a workplace.[5]

A few of the articles were downright scary. According to several—including one in the *Journal of the American Medical Association* and another in *Pediatrics*—one little-discussed problem is the disturbing prevalence of "cytomegalovirus" (CMV). *Pediatrics* reported that about half of the children under three years old in large day care centers have active CMV infections.[6] This virus is often asymptomatic and usually causes nothing worse than minor diarrhea in young children. And yet if these seemingly healthy (or only slightly ill children) transmit the virus to a pregnant woman, it can result in congenital birth defects. Although many women have developed immunities to this virus, some doctors are suggesting that women of childbearing age who come into contact with children in day care—both mothers and child care workers—be tested to see if they are susceptible to CMV.[7]

Those 117 medical articles examined different issues and different diseases and did so with different approaches, but they came to the same general conclusion. Children in day care face increased health risks as compared to children at home with their mothers.

A few of the articles suggested, on a positive note, that day care centers could be places where children learned early about health, and that day care could play a role in children being immunized. But those authors admitted that day care had yet to fulfill that potential.[8]

The more medical research we read, the angrier we became. If current medical journals are reporting such a variety of significant health problems associated with day care, why are none of the popular women's magazines reporting that information? In a day when "informed consent" has become a watchword for both the medical community and consumers, shouldn't the popular media be informing the public of such serious health issues impacting our families and our society, concerning the multibillion-dollar day care industry?

Yet mainstream magazines and newspapers tend to downplay both these medical concerns and the concerns that the child development community has about attachment.

Doesn't the mother in the middle, who is making important life decisions for herself and her children, deserve to know the truth?

Don't Worry, Be Happy?

Instead, in popular magazines, we found articles that talked about "What's Right with Day Care."[9] Or "The Verdict Is In! Kids in Day Care Fare As Well As Kids with Stay-at-Home Moms."[10] One article, by best-selling feminist author Susan Faludi, was entitled "The Kids Are All Right: Research Shows Our Bias against Day Care Is Unfounded."[11]

This last article refers to research done by Alison Clarke-Stewart, and Faludi says that research "found that the social and intellectual development of children in day care was six to nine months ahead of that of children who stayed home." Clarke-Stewart's research is, in fact, *The Chicago Study of Child Care and Development*, first published in 1984.[12]

In looking at the research itself, as published in *Quality in Child Care: What Does Research Tell Us?* a publication of the National Association for the Education of Young Children, we reached a very different conclusion.

The Chicago study compared four types of child care arrangements:

1. care provided by an individual (other than mother) in the child's own home
2. care provided in a family day care home
3. care provided in a full-time child care center
4. care provided in a part-time nursery school program—two and a half hours a day

In the first three types of child care, children were being cared for while their mothers were employed, most in full-time jobs. In the last, the nursery school sample, most of the mothers were not employed.

The study is a complex one, measuring eight categories of developmental competence. One of its conclusions is:

> The differences on the child development measures were strong and statistically significant. Children attending nursery school programs consistently scored higher, especially on assessments of cognitive ability, social knowledge, and sociability with the adult stranger. These children were six to nine months more advanced than children in home care.[13]

Anyone reading the research itself would realize that the term "home care" refers to either nanny-type care or family day care homes, not children cared for at home by their own mothers.

In reality, then, the only children in this study whose mothers were at-home mothers were those children in the nursery schools. These were the children who "consistently scored higher" than the children in the other three forms of day care. Children at home with their mothers and not attending a nursery school were not included in the study at all.

So the original research does not support Faludi's claim that "research indicates that if day care has any long-term effect on children at all, it has made them somewhat more social, experimental, self-assured, cooperative, creative."[14]

In fact, the conclusions of the study are the exact opposite of the ones she reports in her article.

High-Quality Care

In most articles that reassure employed mothers that their children in day care are doing well, a key qualifying phrase is "high-quality day care." And as reported in the University of

Colorado research, children in high-quality day care can "benefit socially and intellectually" compared to children in low-quality day care.

But such articles have little to say to the mother whose only day care choices are one of the six in seven centers that failed to qualify as "high-quality day care."

Even the "high-quality" day care centers were damned with faint praise. Kids in such day care were "just as likely" as children with at-home mothers to: *have friends, get married, have children, and be educated.*[15]

One article cited research in which high-risk children attended a high-quality "preschool" program and had long-term benefits.[16] But such pilot programs tend to be very expensive and difficult to duplicate. And the questionable conclusion drawn seemed to be that the results would also apply to children who were not "high risk."[17]

A day care center described in one of these articles had two gymnasiums and a fenced-in rooftop playground. There were wading pools, rabbits to play with, and "people who love the children all day long."[18] How many mothers have the choice to send their children to such a day care center? Is there one like that in your community? If there were, could *you* afford it?

Are such articles being honest with mothers?

The verdict is hardly in. In truth, it seems the jury has yet to even hear the bulk of the evidence.

As a noted professor of pediatrics, the late Dr. Robert Mendelsohn commented:

> Over the past quarter century, parents have been misled by physicians and others in the field of early childhood education. Instead of pressuring government to throw more money into day care, we pediatricians should instead invest more time and energy into informing parents—and our fellow professionals—of the considerable and continuing medical risks that children face when they are cared for outside the home.[19]

The Socialization Myth

Many advocates of day care point to its benefits. Aren't children in day care more socially and intellectually advanced?

There are several answers to that question. Research in day care is, like the Chicago study mentioned above, often misinterpreted. Too many people confuse nursery school and preschool programs with day care. Nursery schools and preschools are part-time programs, often only one or two days a week; children of at-home mothers are enrolled in these programs for purposes of socialization and education.

Day care, on the other hand, is care for children, full- or part-time, while their mothers are employed. Studies that do not distinguish between nursery schools / preschools and day care are ignoring an important issue.

The Chicago study did find that children who were in day care centers had "greater physical independence from mother."[20]

Is this independence a benefit?

Few mothers want their children to be overly dependent on them. By the time children are school-aged and beyond, growing independence is a valuable trait. But how many mothers truly want their preschool children to be more peer oriented? How many of us want to dilute our influence in the lives and values of our children, at just the point when they are most impressionable and when we as parents can have the most lasting influence in their lives?

One magazine article extolling the benefits of day care cited the story of a five-year-old girl who had been in day care for several years before starting kindergarten. On beginning public school, she felt sorry for her friend, who had never been in day care and who was evidently crying each morning as her mother left her at school. She sympathetically told her mother about this poor child who had never been in day care and didn't know how much fun school could be![21]

The story doesn't tell us how many days that "poor child" cried. But in reading it, we couldn't help but wonder: how many days did the sympathetic child cry when she was first left in day care? By what measure does anyone think that a child is better off having dealt with separation at six weeks or six months (when trust and security are the prime developmental issues) than at six years (when the child is developmentally ready and emotionally equipped for exploration and independence)? Who is truly the "poor disadvantaged child" here?

So Many Children, So Many Day Care Options

Jerri was an office manager at an insurance agency before the birth of her son, Nicky. She felt lucky to get her son into a private day care home. She liked the more homelike atmosphere. But there were problems. The woman who ran the home she'd enrolled Nicky in told Jerri she took only five children. But when Jerri showed up unexpectedly early one afternoon, there were fifteen children in the home.

Jerri launched a search for another day care home. But in the second one, Jerri arrived to pick up Nicky one afternoon and found the owner fast asleep on the living room couch, with children wandering around the home unsupervised. She finally put Nicky into a day care center. But in the center, she never knew when she would see a new face as she picked up her son in the afternoon.

Now Nicky is four years old, and Jerri recently took some time off from work to be with him.

As earlier cited, many mothers like Jerri want "home day care," where someone cares for several children at home. In such a setting, there is apt to be a more family-like atmosphere and one or two consistent caregivers who are there all day, every day. Particularly if a mother can find a friend or relative who is providing child care in her home, this option seems to be the closest to having mother at home with the child.

Family day care homes offer several advantages over other types of day care. In such care, a child has some peers to interact with, without being overwhelmed by the large numbers of children in some centers. The Chicago study found that children in day care homes tend to be more sociable with other children than those in day care centers or those who stayed in their own home with a nanny.[22]

Day care homes provide a more healthy place for preschoolers. In general, a variety of research indicates that the smaller the day care center, the fewer the health problems— with children in small day care homes faring the best.[23]

Other research indicates that the quality of care in family day care homes varies greatly from home to home. Good day care homes are ones where: the caregiver has some education and experience; the caregiver reads often to the children in her care, engages in games and music activities with the children, and talks to them in warm, nonauthoritative ways. And in good day care homes, children watch little television.[24]

But I *Have* to Work!

Readers at this point may be thinking, *But many mothers have to work! . . . I have to work!* Indeed, many women provide the sole or primary financial support for their families. Others have invested considerable time and energy into careers they are reluctant to abandon, even in the interest of their children.

Peggy, the pharmacist you met in chapter 1, knew that she needed to work in order to stay current in her profession. Even a few years away from her job would have meant starting over.

Angela, a nurse who left her career to be at home with her three children, learned that lesson the hard way. She has found it impossible to return to nursing after several years out of the field. She did not realize that her skills would be out of date so quickly.

Selma's husband left her shortly after the birth of their daughter. She was able to stay home with her child for four months, but after that, she told us, "it was work or welfare. And welfare wasn't an option."

There will always be mothers who need help caring for their children. We do not want to heap guilt onto mothers who see no other choices for their lives. But as we'll see in Part III of this book, radical motherhood offers women more options than many of us realize.

What Do Families Need?

Julie is the president of her company. When we asked her what she considered important in her life, she responded:

"My whole life is my son. I need to know that both my husband and I will be able to provide for my son, to the absolute fullest. To give him everything he needs: a good college education; a good base in life; the absolute best. I want to give him everything. Being a mother is the most satisfying thing that I've ever done in my life.

"I love to shop for him. When I go shopping—it's Baby Gap! I love what's new at Baby Gap.

"I wish I could be a stay-home mother. I don't think kids are getting the guidance that they should be getting. I think it is better for children if they have stay-home mothers. But you really don't have an alternative nowadays. It's really hard."

So many mothers work not for a career but in order to make ends meet. And indeed, many mothers work to put food on the table and to pay the rent. And families are under real economic pressure.

But at some level of income—much lower than most people think—families do begin to have a choice.

Too many mothers assume that their children will be OK in day care, that mothers returning to work is just a part of our lives today. And they work to be able to afford clothes from Baby Gap, shoes from Nike, or a big-screen television. Too many of them are saying, with Julie, "I wish I could stay home with my children. I think children do better with stay-at-home moms. But I don't have an alternative."

What Do Mothers Want?

Most observers recognize that our country has a day care crisis. But many children's advocates, including women's activists who address this issue, see a variety of ready solutions: pour more government money into day care; provide better training and higher pay for day care teachers; conduct background checks; and so forth.

But assuming it could be achieved, is more and better day care the solution that most mothers want? The answer to that question has two sides.

The first is reflected in the fact that, in one poll, 72 percent of the employed mothers said that they worked more for financial reasons than for self-fulfillment.[25] And, in another poll, 87 percent of mothers want to spend more time caring for their children.[26] Clearly, most of the mothers in the middle want to find ways to care for their children themselves *and* fulfill their own potential.

The second consideration is to look at the day care choices that employed mothers are already making for their own children.

Perhaps the single most striking (and little-publicized) fact about the current child care choices of employed mothers is that the majority of them choose for their preschool children to be cared for by relatives. This is not immediately apparent in the data: the current population survey divides child care categories according to "place of care" rather than *who* cares for the child.

For instance, there are two categories allocated for care by grandparents: one in the child's home, one in "another home." Care by other relatives—aunts, uncles, and so on—is treated the same way. As a result, the data states that only 35.7 percent of children under five years of age are cared for in their own home.

Let's recategorize that data. Organized by *who* cares for the children of employed mothers, rather than by *place* of care, we find:

28.7 percent are cared for by a parent—either a father at home or a mother at her place of employment

15.8 percent are cared for by grandparents

7.7 percent are cared for by other relatives—aunts, uncles, and so on

23.3 percent are cared for by nonrelatives, in a home setting

15.8 percent are cared for in group day care centers

7.3 percent are cared for in nursery schools and preschools[27]

Almost one-third of children in day care are cared for by their own parents! That indicates efforts by parents to be creative in their work-and-child-care arrangements.

Over half of the children whose mothers are employed are in the care of a family member! This is strong evidence as to what kind of care most employed mothers prefer for their children.

Organized child care—day care centers, nurseries, and preschools—care for less than one in every four children of employed mothers. Nevertheless, it is precisely this organized, out-of-home care that most public policy discussions are tilted toward.

The Real Issues

In general, child care stories in the media, like much of the research used to support day care, tend to ignore or gloss over several important variables. Based on our research and Deborah's more than twenty years in the field of early childhood education, we believe that the real issues any mother in the middle needs to consider in making her own choice about day care for her child are these:

Older is better. Time and again, research on both the health aspect of day care and the attachment aspect found age to be a critical factor. The conclusions were that the older the child, the stronger the immune system and the stronger the attachment to the parents, and therefore the better the child coped with group situations and with separation from the mother.

Part-time is better. The employed mothers we talked to who seemed to be the happiest and most satisfied with life were ones able to work part-time rather than long hours. Which coincides with—and may help explain—the conclusions that children in part-time care also fared better, not so much in terms of illness but in their relationships with their parents.

High-quality care makes a big difference. Much of the day care research is done in university child care centers, where the staff-child ratio is high, conditions are optimal, and there is little sudden staff turnover.

But parents who use research done in good day care centers to reassure themselves that their children will be OK in low-quality care are deceiving themselves. It's true that in numerous studies, centers that were smaller and had good staff-child ratios and low staff turnover, and where teachers developed relationships with their students, were the ones in which children did all right. But parents need to remind themselves that according to the University of Colorado study, that's only one in seven.

Family circumstances are crucial. Children eventually learn what choices their parents are making. In families where mothers truly must work to put food on the table, the children may better understand. On the flip side, our experience has convinced us that children also know if parents are working to buy newer, more expensive cars, a membership in a country club, a new big-screen television, or even a VCR. On some level, they sense that these other things are more important than they are.

Latchkey Children

Up to this point, we have been focusing on the needs of the youngest children caught in the cross fire. But they aren't the only innocent victims of the mommy wars.

Sharon, now a mother of two teenagers, told us she was a latchkey child long before anyone coined that phrase. Her most vivid memories of childhood are of coming home after school to an empty house:

"I would set a chair in the hallway of our house. From that spot, I could see both the front and back doors. And I would sit there, looking from one door to the other, waiting for Mama to come home. Wintertime, when the sun went down early, was the worst. Then I would sit on my chair, in the dark, scared to death, counting the headlights passing in front of the house until my mother's car finally pulled in the driveway. I vowed from those days on that I would never do that to my own children."

Most researchers and child development authorities advise against leaving children to fend for themselves. But many mothers in the middle have few resources for school-age children; day care, after-school activities, and baby-sitters are either not available or not affordable in many areas.

"Though we don't advocate that parents leave kids home alone—and never if a child is under age ten—we have to recognize the need is a modern reality," says Ginny Markell, a vice president of the National PTA.[28]

One result of this modern reality is that we now have millions more home-alone kids like Sharon than we did when she was growing up just a generation ago. Which leads *The Handbook for Latchkey Children and Their Parents*, by child psychologists Thomas Long and his wife, Lynette Long, to warn:

> Even kids who seem to handle the latchkey experience well may sometimes feel fearful, lonely or bored, and resentful of parents. . . . The most common fear for kids home alone is that someone will break in and hurt them.[29]

But loneliness and fear aren't all that latchkey kids have to face. David Elkind's landmark treatment of the topic in *The Hurried Child* spotlighted more sides of this issue than we have time or space to delve into here. Suffice it for us to say that we see many, if not most, hurried children as oft-forgotten victims of, and refugees from, the mommy wars. Like refugees of any war, many of them have been aged beyond their years by experiences, situations, and decisions they were never prepared to face.

According to a study by social scientist Jean Richardson and her colleagues, *eighth-grade students* who took care of themselves for eleven or more hours a week were twice as likely to be abusers of controlled substances (that is, to smoke marijuana or tobacco or to drink alcohol) as those who were actively cared for by adults. The increased risk appeared no matter what the sex, race, or socioeconomic status of the children. And students who took care of themselves for eleven or more hours per week were one and a half to two times more likely "to score high on risk taking, anger, family conflict, and stress" than those who did not care for themselves.[30](Emphasis ours.)

While the media reports from the front line of the mommy wars usually ignore (but sometimes misrepresent) their story, the alarming truth is that children of all ages are caught in the cross fire.

What Is the Answer?

So many "experts" are telling us we need more and better day care. But that isn't what many mothers in the middle are saying. We hear most of them saying:

"I work because I have to."
"I wish I could spend more time with my children."
"I feel better leaving my child with my mother, my husband, my sister."

In unison, the voices of mothers on the front lines of the mommy wars are calling for help in the rescue of their children caught in the cross fire. They're saying, "We need more choices, real choices that don't force us to choose between our children and ourselves."

Nine

The Attack on Motherhood

*For while maternal devotion may be perfectly genuine,
this, in fact, is rarely the case. Maternity is usually a
strange mixture of narcissism, altruism, idle daydreaming,
sincerity, bad faith, devotion, and cynicism. The great danger which threatens the infant in our culture lies in the fact
that the mother to whom it is confided in all its helplessness is almost always a discontented woman: sexually she
is frigid or unsatisfied; socially she feels herself inferior to
man; she has no independent grasp on the world or on the
future. . . . One is frightened at the thought that defenseless
infants are abandoned to her care.*

Simone de Beauvoir, *The Second Sex*, 1952[1]

Say the words: baseball . . . motherhood . . . apple pie. Say
them slowly. Solemnly. Reverently. You can almost hear
"The Star-Spangled Banner" sounding in the background. "As
American as . . ." Motherhood practically has the flag wrapped
around it.

We celebrate Mother's Day with cards, flowers, reverence,
and the ultimate tribute, chocolate. When the 1994 Academy
Award–winning movie *Forrest Gump* infected the country with

Gumpmania, it was partly because audiences so resonated with Forrest's idiot savant, homespun sayings: "My mama always told me ... " The story of a child overcoming handicaps, propelled to greatness by a devoted mother, struck a responsive chord deep in our collective soul.

So why, then, do so many women today feel that they can't say simply, "I'm a mother" with pride? A man can pull out pictures of babies, and peers will ooh and aah appreciatively. Women do so only at risk of rolled eyes and condescending interest.

Where did we get the gender slur "just a housewife?" After all, no male ever says he is "just a businessman" apologetically, as if he were a drag on social productivity, when in fact most men in business work much fewer hours than do most mothers of infants, toddlers, or school-age children.

When it comes to motherhood as an institution in our society, we are suffering from a deep, collective, national schizophrenia. While honoring mothers on the rhetorical level with odes to their role, we devalue them on the practical level by not respecting their jobs.

According to economist Sylvia Hewlett, author of *When the Bough Breaks*, the 1950s were a time of great emphasis on motherhood. She identifies this period, with its stress on mothers' at-home care of their children, as a "cult of motherhood."[2] Everywhere women turned, the culture was recognizing the importance of motherhood.

Well, not quite everywhere. Even though Hewlett and others correctly emphasize how homemaker-oriented the culture was in the fifties, at the same time mothers and motherhood were hearing the opening salvos of what would soon become a vicious and debilitating assault. *The Second Sex*, Simone de Beauvoir's lengthy and influential essay on women's roles, was released in 1952. Her relatively brief chapter on "mothers" focused on abortion and was just as overwhelmingly negative as the quote at the beginning of this chapter indicates.[3]

Mothers are "almost always" discontented and sexually frigid? The attack on motherhood was, by then, well under way.

A Three-Pronged Assault

The "cult of motherhood" in the fifties was actually the second such wave of emphasis on a woman's role at home. In many ways, it was a weak echo of what historians called the "cult of domesticity" or the "cult of womanhood" in the fifties— the 1850s, that is. For while the women of the 1800s had much less freedom and fewer societal rights than their great-granddaughters a century later, the honor accorded them as mothers was much higher. This is largely because the early 1800s were the apotheosis of respect for motherhood before our culture was hit with three major "isms" that have sorely undermined motherhood: Darwinism, professionalism, and feminism.

The most recent attack on motherhood, led by modern feminism, is the most well known to contemporary women. We've already chronicled some of the damage done by Betty Friedan's wrong prescription for the feminine mystique. We've talked about the corresponding devaluing of children in our society. And we've noted the purveyance of this philosophy throughout the media—but especially in women's magazines, which subtly (and sometimes not so subtly) denigrate motherhood while actually deceiving their readers by failing to report the truth about the great body of research on such major motherhood concerns as mother-child attachment issues and day care diseases.

But the deep ambivalence Americans feel about motherhood can only be comprehended if we know that feminism is a latecomer to the war on the value of mothers. The roots of antagonism go much deeper than just the last twenty or thirty years, and it is important to know that. Even our historical terminology is revealing. Why do the names that historians and other observers give to the two times in our history when motherhood was celebrated include the term "cult"?

Darwinism: An Evolutionary Cul-de-Sac

Man has ultimately become superior to woman.

Charles Darwin, *The Descent of Man*, 1871[4]

Imagine for a moment a time when many mothers had eight or more children. Imagine a time before public hospitals and antibiotics, when many children died as infants. Imagine no running water. Imagine washing all clothes by hand—after boiling water on a coal stove. Imagine cooking on a coal stove.

It's not hard to imagine, then, that the hardworking women of a century gone by had little time for anything but children and home. They did not have, as Virginia Woolf pointed out in her famous 1929 speech, "a room of one's own."

At the time Woolf wrote that famous speech, many men believed women were innately inferior to men—some said the lack of significant female achievement proved this point. "I thought of that old gentleman," said Woolf, "who declared that it was impossible for any woman, past, present, or to come, to have the genius of Shakespeare." Woolf replied that without resources, and weighed down by "arduous and difficult struggles," it was impossible for women to write with the brilliance of Shakespeare. Hence the need for "money and a room of one's own."[5]

After the daily struggle to keep everyone in her household fed, warm, dry, and clean, the average mother in the nineteenth century didn't have a lot of time or energy left for thinking great thoughts and dreaming great dreams. This was, however, held against women collectively, as evidence of inferiority.

And by whom? Leading the pack was none other than Charles Darwin:

> The chief distinction in the intellectual powers of the two sexes is shown by man's attaining to a higher eminence, in whatever he takes up, than can woman—whether requiring deep thought, reason or imagination, or merely the use of the senses and hands.[6]

Not only didn't women achieve more but according to the new evolutionary science, they simply couldn't! There were women of achievement, a few who were either wealthy enough or fortunate enough to have opportunities for formal learning, but compared to the number of accomplished men, it was obvious that superior women were not representative of their entire gender. Or so the argument went.

This belief was not new in the nineteenth century; at the time, it was generally accepted that women were inferior to men. But Darwin's contribution to the attack on motherhood was the ratification of science. He gave misogynists and garden-variety chauvinists cover in the war on women, by "explaining" women's alleged inferiority.

Darwin viewed the world as one huge struggle for progress—men pitted against one another *mano a mano*, fighting for mates and societal position, moving society forward in the evolutionary spiral: "survival of the fittest." Women were merely observers and accouterments to the struggle. Historian Glenna Matthews explains, "Male struggle outside the home is the engine of change. Of necessity confined to the home and to nurturing activities, women necessarily carry a biological taint."[7]

Even more important than the entrenchment of the inferiority argument was the direct hit on motherhood. Previously, women in general were believed intellectually inferior. With Darwin's assistance, that inferiority was now specifically tied to motherhood. Strangely, the reproductive capacity of women—which, as women's unique contribution to the human race, had been a reservoir of strength and self-respect—was now redrawn as an evolutionary cul-de-sac.

The thesis was that women's evolutionary energies were used up in the process of conception, pregnancy, and childbirth. Herbert Spencer, a peer of Darwin, postulated that:

> The first set of differences [between the sexes] is that which results from a somewhat earlier arrest of individual evolution in women than in men, necessi-

tated by the reservation of vital power to meet the cost of reproduction.[8]

One might be forgiven the thought that reproduction is a positive, generative, even evolutionary act. But no. To Darwinians and social Darwinians, childbirth merely reproduced mankind—it didn't move society forward. Childbearing maintained the status quo; it was a sort of animalistic treading of water.

Sadly, this devaluing of motherhood was reinforced even by those thinkers who rushed to defend women. For example, Lester Frank Ward, the first president of the American Sociology Society, believed that "the fertile sex is of by far the greater importance." Nevertheless, he argued that she was still inferior to men because she had not had opportunity to better herself due to her domestic duties:

> It is often remarked that women are, as a rule, more frivolous and trifling than men. Being the truth, it may as well be spoken. . . . Where the only objects with which woman comes in contact are those of the kitchen, the nursery, the drawing room, and the wardrobe, how shall she be expected to have broad ideas of life, the world, and the universe?. . . Give woman an interest in great subjects, and she will abandon small ones.[9]

While Ward's point about women's limited sphere of opportunity is well taken—it is essentially the same "room-of-one's-own" argument—he still ends up devaluing motherhood by lumping "the nursery," and by obvious association the children in it, with "small" things that are inconsequential or downright negative, like "gossip, slander, and fashion worship."[10]

But it wasn't just men attacking women. It was here that the opening shots of the mommy wars were fired. Early feminist Charlotte Perkins Gilman, a Darwinian and a student of Ward, was virulently anti-motherhood. She herself experienced a nervous breakdown, following her daughter's birth.

After recovery, she left her husband, eschewed her own maternal duties, and allowed her ex-husband and his new wife to raise her daughter. The daughter of a cold mother, Gilman saw little positive and redeeming value to motherhood. "The 'sacred duties of maternity' reproduce the race," she said, "but they do nothing to improve it."[11]

Gilman held such a dim view of motherhood that she believed children needed teachers, not mothering:

> It may be said in extreme terms that it would be better for a child today to be left absolutely without mother or family of any sort, in the city of Boston, for instance, than to be supplied with a large and affectionate family and to be planted with them in Darkest Africa.[12]

This attack on motherhood provided the bridge to the next wave of attack—from "ism" number two. Gilman was a Darwinian, but she was also an influential Progressive, and her writings laid the groundwork for the damage that turn-of-the-century reformers unwittingly did to motherhood with the advent of . . .

Professionalism

The 1900s brought the Progressive movement, with its faith in the knowledge and superiority of the expert. Professionalism was the rage as every facet of life came under the analysis of science and the standard of efficiency.

Not surprisingly, mothers soon received their share of scrutiny. Motherhood had always been down to earth and intuitive, with skills taught from mother to daughter. Nothing so haphazard for the Progressives! Being a modern mother now required the advice of professionals.

In 1914 the federal government began putting out a twenty-five-cent pamphlet entitled *Infant Care*, which instructed mothers in scientific child-rearing. It quickly became the

Government Printing Office's best-selling publication.[13] Scientific advice on proper mothering proliferated, and in 1926 *Parents* magazine appeared.

But underneath this flurry of advice for mothers was the assumption that women needed help. This attitude reflected a fundamental devaluing of the mother-housewife's expertise. The Progressive's professionalism, disguised as scientific progress for motherhood, was—at its heart—still a paternalistic attack on motherhood.

A good example is the 1914 book aptly titled *Increasing Home Efficiency*, by Martha and Robert Breure:

> It is a desirable condition based on knowledge of housekeeping—ordered knowledge gained from experts in school, and in startling contrast to the wisdom of "mother," who was equipped for the business of teaching with nothing better than tradition, devotion to her home, humility as to what she had a right to demand in the way of mechanical assistance or financial compensation, and especially with a firm and disastrous conviction that her own experience, however limited, was an infallible guide.[14]

Professionalism was an escalation of the mommy wars: the efficiency experts speaking down to housewives from on high were not generally men but a new class of professional women. Rising educational opportunities for women at this time far outstripped professional opportunities. As a result, educated women were, by and large, still confined to the "women's sphere" of hearth and home.

This gave rise to the home economics movement, which gave well-trained women scientists a place in society to exercise their talents. Unfortunately, as Matthews comments, these women needed to "denigrate housewives in order to set themselves apart from their sisters and thereby define themselves as worthy of inclusion among male professionals."[15]

It turns out that sister vs. sister is nothing new.

Smother Love

From there—"Mom needs expert advice"—it was down-hill to "Mom is dangerous!" The experts began preaching that mother love was smother love; maternal attention just wasn't, well, scientific enough. According to one of these experts, pediatrician Luther Emmet Holt, even breast-feeding was "unscientific."[16]

This was the beginning of behaviorism, and its primary proponent, John B. Watson, counseled mothers to be very careful about being too affectionate toward their children:

> If you must, kiss them once on the forehead when they say good night. Shake hands with them in the morning. . . . Remember, when you are tempted to pet your child, that mother love is a dangerous instrument! An instrument which may inflict a never-healing wound which may make infancy unhappy, adolescence a nightmare . . . an instrument which may wreck your adult son or daughter's vocational future and their chances for marital happiness.[17]

Mothers were simply too emotional; children needed discipline and stoicism.

The evidence? In 1943 David Levy cited "maternal over-protection" as a major problem showing up in the psychological testing of young men headed for service in World War II. These young men, he said, were unfit for service because of "smother love."[18]

Clearly, mothers were a problem.

This same basic mind-set—that women need expert help to more efficiently fulfill their traditional roles, that science can improve on maternal instincts, and that "newer" is always an improvement over age-old traditions—had a profound impact on what had previously been the almost exclusively female spheres of childbirth and maternity care.

The same "progressive" thinking touted man-made formula as a marvelously modern scientific advancement over natural mother's milk and soon went on to revolutionize the childbirth arena by taking it from the hands of midwives and making it an overwhelmingly male-dominated medical specialty. While obstetrics developed medical technology that saved the lives of many high-risk babies, there was a downside. Modernized medicine subjected all women to increasingly intrusive procedures, until it reached a point a generation ago where laboring women were routinely anesthetized so that the actual birth could be "performed" by expert medical personnel.

Our generation's growing appreciation for the benefits of natural childbirth has helped restore women's traditional sense of ownership and involvement in the childbirth arena. But some residue of past paternalism remains.

There has been a backlash against natural childbirth in some areas on the part of some medical practitioners. And more than a few members of the medical community seem to reserve their most patronizing treatment for pregnant women, maternity patients, and mothers of young children.

We are now two or three generations removed from a time when childbirth and maternity care were a natural part of women's sphere of life. As a result, most modern mothers have never attended any birth other than their own. Without such traditional experience or exposure, millions of women today take their first uncertain (and sometimes fearful) steps into the world of motherhood doubting their own maternal instincts and, unfortunately, feeling insecure and inadequate as mothers. So in this way, even modern medicine has inadvertently contributed to the devaluing of motherhood.

Feminism

> Bringing up children is not a real occupation because children come up just the same, brought or not.
>
> Germaine Greer[19]

Despite such broad-scale societal attacks over the years, motherhood remained an all-American institution. And it came roaring back in the late forties and early fifties—after the end of the war. Everything was booming: the economy, marriage, the suburbs, and of course, the national birth rate. This was the era of the much-maligned Ozzie and Harriet, and Ward and June Cleaver.

As a nation, we'd been down a long road to happiness and prosperity through one depression and two world wars. As if in celebration of their survival, Americans resumed their pursuit of the American dream with joyous abandon, working to rebuild hearth and home at every turn and on every suburban corner lot.

But underneath the boom were the beginnings of a bust. Many were happy; some were not.

The suburbs were, for many, an opportunity to establish happy homes in neighborhoods where children could play in safety. Others there lived lives of anonymous isolation. The rise of the commute for husbands left some wives lonely in their increasingly separate lives. As we noted in chapter 2, the rise of the modern household, with its amazing timesaving devices, left some women bored and devoid of work satisfaction; the rise of consumerism left their lives bereft of purpose.

Enter Betty Friedan's *The Feminine Mystique* in 1963 to speak for these women, and a movement was born. Unfortunately, once again, motherhood was under attack. Women were ridiculed for having "a love affair with their own children."[20]

But that proved to be just the beginning. The attack only gathered steam from there. Another feminist compared the full-time care of a baby to "spending all day, every day, in the exclusive company of an incontinent mental defective."[21]

The assault on motherhood heated up as even *Playboy*, a seemingly unlikely ally of feminists, joined the fray by mocking the housewife and belittling her role with this parody of a job notice in the classifieds:

Tired of the Rat Race?

Fed up with Job Routine?

Well, then ... how would you like to make $8,000, $20,000—as much as $50,000 and more—working at home in your Spare Time? No selling! No commuting! No time clocks to punch.

BE YOUR OWN BOSS!!!

Yes, an Assured Lifetime Income can be yours now, in an easy, low-pressure, part-time job that will permit you to spend most of each and every day as you please.[22]

The Feminist Shift

As we turned the corner into the seventies, the discussion of women became increasingly oriented toward reproduction (not to be confused with motherhood). Shulamith Firestone, a fiery twenty-five-year-old feminist, wrote in 1970 that the "first demand" of women should be to free themselves "from the tyranny of their reproductive biology by every means available and the diffusion of the childbearing and child-rearing role to society as a whole."[23] Increasingly, the discussion of women's reproductive capacities did not revolve around (or even involve) motherhood. Instead, it became almost obsessively sexualized.

Pulitzer Prize–winning poet and feminist Anne Sexton wrote "In Celebration of My Uterus" in 1969, " in celebration of the woman I am, and of the soul of the woman I am."[24] But in truth, the soul was stripped.

The very nature of motherhood changed subtly, almost imperceptibly. Firestone's first demand was materializing. Pregnancy and childbirth were no longer part of the mysterium of life, existing on an entirely different plane: they had devolved into another life choice, to be managed, planned, and controlled. Irony of ironies: abortion transferred pregnancy solidly into the "woman's sphere." Out of men's control, yes—but also out of his care.

This is about the point at which the feminine mystake and the attack on motherhood met and mutated into a very different species of feminism. The whole tenor of the times was one of revolution—women needed to be liberated from an oppressive patriarchal system and freed from their biological destiny.

In her insightful book *Who Stole Feminism?* feminist professor Christina Hoff Sommers chronicles this critical philosophical shift by distinguishing between two waves of feminism.[25] The historic and first wave—or "equity" feminists, as she names them—wanted for women what they wanted for everyone: fair treatment, without discrimination. She quotes Elizabeth Cady Stanton, who addressed the New York State Legislature in 1854, saying, "We ask no better laws than those you have made for yourselves. We need no other protection than that which your present laws secure to you."

In contrast, this latest contemporary wave of feminism argues that women are still oppressed in a system of male domination that exploits and humiliates them. They believe that women and men are engaged in a gender war. That women should be loyal only to other women and on their guard against the men in their lives. That women should be discouraged from pursuing a "housewife track." That a utopian world would be one without gender at all, where women wouldn't be handicapped by such biologically limiting roles as childbirth and nursing. Many of the current feminist writers and speakers are what Sommers calls "sex-gender" feminists.

Sommers, herself an outspoken feminist, believes that this second wave of feminism "is socially divisive and . . . lacks a constituency among American women."[26]

Indeed, we—like most women we know—agree with the first philosophy of feminism but not the second. While most of us believe that women should have equal opportunity for jobs and education, and equal treatment under the law, few women want to wage war with the men in their lives. Few mothers view their sons as future oppressors of their daughters.

Yet the far-reaching impact of the sex-gender feminist view of the world shows up in little ways. New school textbooks rarely portray romance, marriage, or motherhood in positive ways. Books that have pictures of women holding babies are considered stereotypical and are frowned on. Motherhood, that experience that many women find to be an exhilarating, defining moment of their lives, is viewed as capitulation to a system of male dominance. In this perspective, mothers are prisoners, children our chains, and men the cruel jailers.

Feminist Everywoman vs. The Mother in the Middle

> No woman should be authorized to stay at home to raise her children. . . . Women should not have that choice, precisely because if there is such a choice, too many women will make that one.
>
> Simone de Beauvoir,
in an interview with Betty Friedan[27]

The most obvious flaw in the gender-feminist philosophy is this: most women don't (and never did) want to be liberated from their children. Thus, much of the current popular debate, framed as it is in glass ceiling terms, does not reflect reality for the mother in the middle. There is often a mythic theme in the public discussion about women, work, and motivation, a theme that reflects both the original feminine mystake and the crux of the newer gender-feminist belief: the underlying assumption being that women *want* to be freed from motherhood in order to work.

But what is heard more frequently from women themselves is that they *have* to work. Certainly, there are more opportunities for women today, and women have made impressive gains in their professional careers. But for the vast majority of women, paid employment is another responsibility they've shouldered in addition to raising their children. Perhaps this is the most fundamental attack on motherhood, because it is so subtle: there are self-absorbed Noras and Joanna Kramers out there, but for most women, work isn't about self-actualization.

A significant majority of women—62 percent—still make less than $15,000 a year.[28] This is a far cry from economic empowerment. Some of these women, like most men, may be in low-paying but highly fulfilling professions of their choice— writing poetry, for instance—but it is far more likely that they are working at McDonald's and Kmart. Clearly, the majority of employed American women are laboring as wage earners rather than pursuing careers. Indeed, if we go on up the pay scale, we find that 81 percent of women work for less than $25,000 a year.[29]

Why do they work? In 1990 the Roper organization did a survey and asked women themselves. The answer that came back from 3,000 women was a solidly economic one. "Something interesting to do" as a reason for working came in a dismal fourth, behind "supporting self and family" and "making extra money."[30] Then, in May 1995, a Louis Harris survey of 1,502 women found that 55 percent of employed women provide half or more of their household's income: 18 percent provide all; 11 percent provide more than half; and 26 percent provide about half of the family income.[31]

The percentage of women in the workforce laboring out of need appears to be increasing: a 1995 Roper Starch Inc. and Virginia Slims opinion poll of 3,000 women found that 72 percent of employed women say they would have a hard time economically if they didn't work. This was an increase from 57 percent in 1985.[32]

Nevertheless, the women-and-work debate continues to be driven by rhetoric that assumes the workplace is where women want to be. Do they? Many do. But not all. A 1995 poll commissioned by the Merck Family Fund and reported in *Working Woman* found that 87 percent of women say they want to spend more time caring for their children.[33] Roper Starch found that

43 percent of employed women with children would prefer to stay home, while only 33% of women at home would prefer to have a job.[34] Even more significant is the finding that what women really want is part-time work and flextime.[35]

Advances . . . or Retreats?

Most women—87 percent—want to spend more time caring for their children! The march for women's rights continues on, banners unfurled, decidedly ignoring this fact. What do the banners scream? *Day care!* Sometimes it seems that those calling for radical change have only this one note to sing.

Who is working in support of those millions of women who want to be with their children? Perhaps, like de Beauvoir, the feminist activists are afraid too many women will make that choice.

Even those decrying the child care system end up advocating more day care. A recent book, *Other People's Children* by Julia Wrigley, chronicles the problems of nannies and child care, and the sorrow of turning one's children over to strangers for the better part of the day—and still ends up recommending government-regulated day care centers.[36]

This is another facet of the attack on motherhood—the idea that day care is the top priority for America's mothers.

Another questionable goal of the women's movement is the rather recent call for employers to accommodate women who want to use breast pumps at work. Some women are using their breaks to squat in cramped bathroom stalls, others are relegated to storeroom closets—all so that they can "breast-feed" their babies. Let's think this through. Yes, there's lots of evidence showing the benefits of breast milk over formula. But do we really believe a mother's milk is vital but her presence is merely optional?

Before the revolution goes much further, don't we need to stop and ask, Is this an advance . . . or a retreat? Isn't there a higher vision of motherhood we should be working for?

We believe the mommy wars have gone on long enough. We've seen too many innocent victims. It's time for those of us closest to the action, the mothers in the middle, to call a cease-fire, honestly rethink the issues, and help set the peace terms we're willing to accept.

It's time all of us as mothers—at-home moms and employed moms alike—begin constructing a fair, reasonable, and comprehensive plan for achieving a peace our daughters and granddaughters can live with in the next millennium.

PART III:

Searching for Peace

Ten

Revaluing Mothers: How Do We Start?

There is a broader, not a higher, life outside.

Antoinette Brown Blackwell,
The Sexes Throughout Nature, 1875[1]

If it matters to no one else, motherhood matters to our children. In the hustle and bustle of our busy mother-in-the-middle lives, we tend to forget that simple truth. The value of a mother is based on the enduring, unchanging fact that absolutely nothing—nothing—can replace her.

It took the Blizzard of '96 to remind Arianna Huffington how important she is to her children. Arianna, the wife of multimillionaire Michael Huffington, quite literally has all the money in the world to shower on her daughters. But what do they want? They want her:

> As I was putting my four-year-old to bed on the night of the third day of no school, and no baby-sitters who could brave the weather to our home, Isabella said, with her eyes half closed: "You see, Mommy? My New Year's wish was that you would stop working. And God made it happen."

With the magical thinking of a four-year-old, the blizzard was created to keep Isabella's mommy with her all the time.[2]

Heading into the Twenty-First Century

Motherhood has always mattered to children.

But it must be revalued by the rest of us. As we move into the next millennium, our search for peace needs to reframe the women-work-family debate. With the clarification of an appropriate historical perspective, we needn't persist in the presumption that progress for women consists of merely continuing the march into full-time workforce participation—currently defined as employment outside the home.

We're at a crossroads. Will we compound the feminine mystake and continue marching toward the wrong goal post, playing by the rules of the wrong game? Or will we find a new, revolutionary system of work and family that enables mothers to be with their children?

Over two decades ago Jessie Bernard wrote, in *The Future of Motherhood*, that "the reintegration of the roles of mother and worker constitutes one of our major priorities today, an ethical as well as a political imperative."[3]

And yet twenty years later the spheres of work and motherhood continue to be far apart.

If we choose to advance a real revolution to create a new world order that brings the realms of work and motherhood together, where do we start? The battle must be joined on three different levels: families and communities need to work to revalue motherhood; the business world needs to reconstruct its image of the ideal worker; and public policy must become more family oriented.

Family and Community

Revaluing is a difficult concept, because it is so ephemeral—where do we start? Revaluing motherhood begins at the individual level. It begins at home. In chapter 1 we asked, "Where are we in context?" Motherhood must be valued within the context of family and community. We have to begin recognizing the contribution mothers make as a leavening agent in our society.

Susan and her husband, Doug, have five daughters. Raising them on one salary has been difficult for them, but they have always been committed to Susan being at home, even when "it was hard just to afford diapers." When she became pregnant with their first daughter, Doug was still in graduate school. So they moved to a "tiny little apartment" in a less-than-desirable neighborhood, and Doug switched to night school and took a full-time job so that Susan could quit her job when the baby was born.

That was fourteen years ago now, and Susan says they would do it all over again. Perhaps one of the reasons she feels that way is that Susan has been very creative in her motherhood experience. One of the things she did along the way that she remembers most proudly is a play group she and some friends put together.

But not just any old play group. "None of us had big houses," explained Susan, "so we started going to nursing homes for play groups. We thought it would be great for the kids and great for the people in the homes to just get together once a week and have a play group in their big day room."

Soon the group had grown quite large. Not surprisingly, for the elderly people in the home the weekly visits were "a big highlight in their life."

There are many such creative ideas of real worth—worth that goes far beyond a price tag—that mothers contribute back to their community. Recognizing the importance of their everyday, essential contributions—such as volunteering in things like the PTA, a United Way drive, a church's community outreach ministry—is a first step in revaluing motherhood.

What would a restoration of the value of motherhood look like in our society today? It might begin with providing more "psychic income" to women working at home.

Psychic Income

Why does anyone work anyway? Of course, for starters we work for money so that we can buy the things we need and want. But there are actually two kinds of income: economic income and psychic income.

Although some wouldn't, most healthy people would work in some capacity even if it weren't for the money. That's because we get a lot of gratification out of work. There are many elements of psychic income. We work to be productive, to take pride in a job well done, or to develop expertise. We work for personal validation, to be told we did a good job. We work, too, for companionship; we make our friends at work. It's important to many of us to be part of a team, to have shared vision, to be pulling together toward a common goal.

Think for a minute about these elements of psychic income. For the most part, in our society they have largely disappeared from the job of mothering. Mothers today are working isolated and alone, doing a job that is repetitive and whose results are difficult to identify. Mothers must wait years before they can take pride in a job well done. No one gives them periodic positive job reviews. They don't have companionship, and they aren't part of a team. Rather than receiving kudos to compensate for these job challenges, mothers are greeted with awkward silences at dinner parties. The icon for the woman of the nineties is a designer briefcase.

Mother-Friendly Environment?

One mother, Andrea, told us about a particularly bad experience she had while still on maternity leave. Her husband, Doug, wanted her to bring their new baby son into his office so that he could show him off. She did . . . and they got a shocking reaction:

"I walked in and some of the people were looking at him, and they called this one woman over, and she walked right past and didn't say anything. Someone said, 'Hey, you didn't stop to look at the baby.' And she responded, 'Oh, I hate babies.' Then she turned around and walked off. And everyone gasped. She made her point: babies aren't a part of normal office protocol. And she wasn't going to have anything to do with it."

Most of the moms we talked to felt the same devaluing of themselves and their children—though usually in more subtle ways. Few people just come right out and say it. Often, though, the silence is worse.

One way to show mothers they are appreciated would be to construct a more mother-friendly environment in our communities. Psychologist and child development expert Penelope Leach has written that "if anybody cared, there are innumerable things that could be done to make [the lives of mothers and small children] easier and more fun. Many of them would cost nothing." Her imaginative list of mother-friendly ideas includes coming up with a gadget that would hold open doors and elevators while strollers go through, and more changing facilities for babies in public places.[4]

Lillian, a mother of three toddlers, told us she would welcome a more mother-friendly community, because:

"You don't have the neighborhood you had when I grew up. People don't open their doors to just anyone. Even if they are friendly and very nice, as my neighbors are, they still are not available or around. . . . If there were more openness, more support, more 'Hey, come on in' . . . but it's not that way. Everything is so structured and organized. Kids have to be in organized soccer. . . . Here you are in your car—driving around—that's very stressful. My mom just let us out the door, and off we went to play kick the can. We found our own groups, made our own rules. . . . A more open-door policy in neighborhoods would help."

Most of all, we need to find ways to end the isolation. We must reformulate motherhood as a less isolated, more interconnected endeavor in our culture. As Jessie Bernard pointed out, solitary confinement is not good for mothers or children. And it's a crazy way to raise kids:

> The way we institutionalize motherhood in our society—assigning sole responsibility for child care to the mother, cutting her off from the easy help of others in an isolated household, requiring round-the-clock tender, loving care, and making such her exclusive activity—is not only new and unique but not even a good way for either women or—if we accept as a criterion the amount of maternal warmth shown—for children. It may, in fact, be the worst. It is as though we had selected the worst features of all the ways motherhood is structured around the world and combined them to produce our current design.[5]

One mother who told us her story had gone back to work when her first child was almost two years old. She and her husband decided that he would be the one to stay home with their son. But that only lasted three months. "I can't do this," he finally admitted. "I feel so isolated—I've got to get out and get a job. I don't care if it's low paying. I'll go nuts if I stay home all the time."

That's precisely the problem felt by many new moms who have no support network and who cope with caring for a baby in a neighborhood that is largely abandoned each day from morning to night.

Business

Alicia and Jerry were very comfortable. Neither one made a lot of money; she worked in a bank, and he managed a retail store at the local mall. But with two incomes, they were able to buy a nice house in a good neighborhood, and they even had a swimming pool.

They just assumed things would always be that way. Alicia's mother always worked when she was little, so Alicia never thought she'd do anything else. Until she had a baby.

The first day back at work full-time after four months maternity leave was very strange for Alicia. "My boss never even asked me about how things were going or how the baby was doing," she said. "Never even mentioned it. He acted like I had never even been on maternity leave. He didn't even ask to see a picture of the baby."

But then it got worse. Alicia lived only five minutes from the bank, so the baby-sitter was able to bring the baby to see her at lunchtime. Alicia consoled herself that at least she would be able to continue breast-feeding and see her baby in the middle of the day.

That lasted just three days before she was called into her boss' office and told she wasn't allowed to do that—it was unsanitary and customers wouldn't like it. "People could bring dogs into the bank that pee on the floor, but I couldn't breast-feed my baby in a locked supply room," commented Alicia. "Then they said it was a security hazard: somebody might know there's a baby coming every day and might come in and rob the bank, taking me and the baby hostage."

It took only two weeks before Alicia realized, "I just couldn't do it. . . . I just couldn't do it." She switched to part-time; they sold their house, and eventually Alicia quit her job entirely.

Unlike Alicia, when Madeline became pregnant, she assumed she would stop working. But unexpectedly, her husband, Ben, said he was interested in staying home with the baby part-time.

They decided to try having both of them work part-time. Madeline worked as a magazine editor, and her bosses readily agreed that she would work four hours every day. Eventually the magazine hired another mother part-time so that she and Madeline could job share.

Madeline loves it. She was even able to continue nursing her daughter until she was a year old, because the four-hour period away meant she only missed one feeding a day. "Working part-time is wonderful," says Madeline. "Those four hours a day when I am at work are stressful, and there are things there that require my full attention. But it's still like a vacation from housework and the demands of a toddler. I have so much more patience when I am at home, because I've had four hours a day, five days a week, off from child care."

Jerry's company was also very flexible and cut his office hours back to twenty hours a week. He freelances the other twenty hours from home, working while the baby is napping and in the evenings. His company, however, was so anxious to keep him that they decided to run his freelance bills through the company payroll so that he still receives full-time benefits.

Their situation enables Madeline, Jerry, and their daughter to be home together as a family, even when one of them is doing at-home work.

"Our situation is almost like a fairy tale," said Madeline. "I know that most women don't have it as pleasurably as I do. Is it wonderful or what!"

The Times They Are A-Changin'

We are at the beginning of a labor revolution as significant as the Industrial Revolution. The labor system will change drastically as a result of the explosive growth of computer and telecommunication technology: the question now is, How will it change?

Will we have more Alicias who experience frustration in their attempts to mesh motherhood with their family needs? Her husband is now working two jobs to support their family. When she became pregnant the second time, he had to be hospitalized briefly for what the doctors concluded was a stress-related illness.

Or will we have more Madelines? She commented that motherhood had slowed down her career because she couldn't be in a management position, but that's a trade-off she's willing to make for now. She also sees how motivated she and the woman she job shares with are. "The company is getting my best four hours of work. I have more energy, more fresh ideas, more creativity. . . . My work is higher quality than when I was full-time. I didn't expect that."

Can we find a better way to reunite the workplace and the home—specifically, the rearing of children? As we found in chapter 2, throughout most of history, women's work and child-rearing were completely integrated in the larger community. Researcher Judith Brown observed, in studying how food was obtained in the preindustrial community, that women's work was based upon the "compatibility of this pursuit with the demands of child care."[6]

This is where we must restart the discussion of women and work. Unfortunately, today's debate—the mommy wars—is almost always phrased in terms of whether women *should* work (as if at-home mothering were not working), instead of discussing where and how. And further, the debate around child care is almost always phrased in terms of how to maximize the mother as worker, in what we believe is a cowardly capitulation to market forces run amok.

Reintegrating work and home, within the expanded parameters of the Technological Revolution, might mean developing a workplace that is flexible—as much as possible for both men and women. The terms of peace may need to include answers like more part-time opportunities, job sharing, working at home, and entrepreneurial ventures.

———————

Remember Sylvia's story from chapter 3? She was the "give everything 110 percent" Madison Avenue executive and mother of three whose life began unraveling when she realized she couldn't be "an A+ player in everything I do. I either had to be a mediocre player at work or a mediocre mom and a mediocre wife. I wasn't willing to settle for that. I decided something in my life had to give."

Well, Sylvia finally decided her professional life could wait. Her kids could not.

The pleasant surprise was that her company wanted her on whatever terms she would agree to. They settled on an arrangement whereby she would be consulted on specific projects part-time and would come into the office three days a week. Which works well for Sylvia and her family.

It's not perfect. Sylvia still has to come to peace with not being a player anymore. "I don't know what I'll do down the road. Right now my focus is on the family, and that's really where it needs to be." Nevertheless, her company wants her to come back and has offered Sylvia her old position part-time, two or three days a week. She's not ready for that, but it's reassuring to know that the option is there. "They treat me like the queen bee when I come in," she says.

That's part of the feminine power we have at our disposal: our talent. Some of the women we talked with were heartened to find they had more leverage—and more options—than they realized because they had skills the marketplace needs. One mother who works from her home commented that she has kept some of her clients because "I have worked very hard to become very good at what I do and to build up my contacts." That's market power we can be using to revolutionize the way the twenty-first century works.

Reintegrating Baby with Work

Lastly, we should be using our market power to achieve a paradigm shift in the workplace: not only must motherhood and work be reintegrated but we need to reverse our cultural bias against integrating children into the workplace.

Children can't be at all workplaces all the time, but it could become more common and more accepted for children to be more than rare or occasional visitors. The horrible abuses of child labor in the nineteenth century and the rise of a more formal workplace have left us with a strict separation between children and work. But maybe there's middle ground to be carved out here, too.

Vivian had just had her third child when she told us she has taken her two older children, ages three and five, with her to meetings. "Usually people are very astounded. They say, 'Wow! My kids would never do that.' I say, 'I don't have an option,'" Vivian explained. "I bring the kids to meetings—they have paper and pencils, they sit and work quietly while I talk." She then went on, "When I was pregnant, I took the kids while I did a major presentation. People came up and said, 'That was great. How can you do this when you are expecting a baby and have two little ones?' You just do it."

Penelope Leach points out that child care as we now practice it has evolved into a "sole task of the moment" endeavor for whomever is doing it, rather than being integrated with the caretaker's other adult responsibilities, and this is not entirely healthy. She notes:

> Separation of parents' work from children's care means that children have lost their taken-for-granted presence in, and apprenticeship to, what adults see as the most important aspect of their lives. Instead of

spending much of childhood watching, "helping," and emulating a range of adult people doing adult things, Western children spend it in special environments designed to keep them out of harm's and adults' way: children's worlds, staffed by people—mostly women....

Such a complete separation of children from the work that structures and absorbs so much of adult life may be a mixed blessing both for children themselves and for society. Play and education are indeed crucial to the development and self-fulfillment of individuals, but it is toward adulthood that children develop and into adult society that they must eventually be integrated.[7]

Certainly we don't have all the strategies for this reintegration, but we know that it should become part of society's discussion about work and family issues.

Perhaps the discussion at a national level will be furthered by Congressman Bill Orton (D-Utah). His son, eight-month-old William "Will" Harvey Orton II, interrupted Shimon Peres' address to a joint session of Congress with an impromptu "Amen!" Unfortunately, those sitting around the two Ortons thought his pronouncement of approval sounded suspiciously like a baby cry. Orton gave Will a bottle, and Congresswoman Zoe Lofgren (D-Calif.), obviously skilled in baby diplomacy, distracted him with her beaded necklace. The speech continued.

Will's dad is unrepentant. Orton persists in bringing Will with him to Capitol Hill about twice a week, even though his wife quit her job as a lobbyist when the baby was born. The picture accompanying an article about Will shows him attending a banking committee meeting in his stroller. In fact, his very first trip—at two days old—was a detour on the way home from the hospital to the floor of the House of Representatives for a vote with his dad.

The congressman told the *Washington Post:* "I want to be Will's dad. And this is the way it works for me. . . . I don't have evenings and weekends to spend with my child. So I do what my schedule and job allows me to do. Everyone has to do that. Many Americans have difficulty meeting those two obligations. Life for me, as for everyone else, is a conflict of priorities."[8]

Would a congresswoman have received the same positive, respectful coverage in the press? She should. But it's doubtful.

Before she got married, Andrea (who had the encounter with the baby-hating woman) thought that "career was my thing." She held a very prominent position as a lobbyist in Washington, D.C., for a nonprofit advocacy group. The fact that she believes wholeheartedly in the issues she works on magnified her devotion to her career. So it was not without struggle that she came to the decision to quit her job after the arrival of her son. "I feel very strongly," she said, "that anyone can do my job, but no one else can raise my son."

Her boss, however, had other ideas. "Mark, my supervisor, approached me with the idea [of a flexible schedule], and he has at least one other person currently on the same schedule," she explained. "He found it was a way to help the organization maintain consistency. When you have a high turnover with women having babies and leaving, you just can't have continuity. So he thought a flexible plan that kept me working was a plus." Andrea agreed she would work twenty hours a week, primarily from home but with two afternoons a week in the office.

The most innovative part of the arrangement, however, is that the baby is welcome in the office. "My organization is very baby friendly," Andrea explained. "There are other mothers who have children of various ages wandering around the office." The office reaction to her motherhood, Andrea said, was "almost unanimously positive—in particular, in my own department. I am overwhelmed by the attention my son gets in the office. Sometimes so many people want to come in and help that it is too much."

It's not a perfect arrangement—she once had to call back to her office when she got caught in a hearing on Capitol Hill, to make sure that someone would feed the baby on time. Admittedly, there are times when the baby is distracting to her and her colleagues. But the arrangement is a trailblazing effort. Andrea said that when she and her boss were discussing the original agreement, "I told him that if it didn't work for me at home with the baby, or if it didn't work to the benefit of the office, I would quit." But that hasn't been necessary. "So far, I think we are both getting a good deal," she concluded.

Others too have made bringing babies to the office work. John Sawyer and Eric Yaverbaum are partners of Jericho Promotions, a public relations firm in New York City. When both were thirty-three, their wives had babies six weeks apart. For the next three years, their children came to work with their dads every day.

Like Andrea, they found that it wasn't perfect but was still worth it. "When I hear my daughter, Cole, crying—no matter what I'm doing, I drop it," Eric says. "I've been on the phone with presidents of major corporations, and she comes in and wants to play jacks. She doesn't really understand the 'shhh-hush' sign. Nor does the person on the other end of the phone. But we clearly choose our priorities here."[9]

Constructing the Ideal Worker

Is it possible that fathers as well as mothers might benefit in a creative and comprehensive peace settlement of the mommy wars? Could we reach a point where the good family man *and* the good family woman are reinstituted as an ideal? Why shouldn't attention to one's family be considered a social necessity and a prerequisite for advancement in business? The biblical prescription is that a leader must be a person with a well-attended family; what if we adhered to that?[10]

Let's envision a situation in which, when an employer notices that a worker who has school-age children has never taken an afternoon off to attend a school function or a parent-teacher conference, the employer becomes concerned—rather than the current situation, in which not allowing personal family issues to impinge on work at all is considered a badge of honor.

Who made the law that a child's voice in the background of a phone call is unprofessional?

Feminist author Joan C. Williams writes persuasively that the problem facing society (and women in particular) is that it is impossible to be both an ideal worker and a parent. Neither men nor women can win in the game of business if they take their parenting responsibilities seriously:

> Western wage labor is premised on an ideal worker with no child care responsibilities. . . . Society is structured so that everyone, regardless of sex, is limited to two unacceptable choices—men's traditional life patterns or economic marginality. Under the current structure of wage labor, people are limited to being ideal workers, which leaves them with inadequate time to devote to parenting, and being primary parents condemned to relative poverty (if they are single parents) or economic vulnerability (if they are currently married to an ideal worker). Wage labor does not have to be structured in this way.[11]

No, it doesn't have to be structured that way. As we enter a new millennium, our generation has a historic opportunity to change our wage labor system—and yet the debate seems to be running down a tired old groove that holds no promise of real change for the mother in the middle. Williams points out, as few feminists are willing to do, that the day care agenda actually consigns women to continued marginalization. Moth-

208 Mother in the Middle

ers with children in day care are still unable to work as late and as long and travel as often as most businesses expect their fast-track employees to do. Not to mention the inevitable childhood illnesses.

Industrialization brought us the modern separation of home and work. But it also brought us unprecedented progress and prosperity. Perhaps technology can bring us back full circle.

Skeptics may counter that there are professions that don't lend themselves well to flexible arrangements. Medicine and the law, for instance. Nevertheless, the contrarian impulse in us wants to issue the challenge: why not?

After all, it's not just mother-doctors and mother-attorneys who are struggling with the crushing demands of their professions. There are far too many men whose lives have been shipwrecked by the traditional round-the-clock requirements of a medical career, and too many men who have seen their families disintegrate in their pursuit of the partner track at their law firm.

Who says it has to be that way? It's time to start a real revolution. A fast-track career is not what most mothers are calling for. Full-time employment for all mothers is hardly a crusade most women want to join. Calling for more and "better" day care is a weak substitute for authentic reformation.

Public Policy

Although we must start revaluing motherhood within the family, at the cultural level, and in the business world, that's not all that must be done. It's not sufficient. Our public policies must also become more family friendly and reflect our valuation of motherhood as an important and essential American institution. We see four specific areas of public policy that must be reformed: divorce laws and practice, the day care agenda, tax policy, and welfare policy.

Any one of these areas can have, and has had, whole books written about it, so this is meant to be the briefest of surveys.

We include it because the mother in the middle must care what happens at the policy formulation level (national, state, and community): our public policies are merely reflections of what our culture values. Right now we are saying quite plainly, through our policies, that we don't value motherhood.

Divorce Reform

One reason there has been such a mass movement of mothers into the marketplace is the insecurity of marriage in our society. A marriage contract is the most worthless legal contract you can sign in our country today. To benefit both mothers and fathers, the institution of no-fault divorce must be reformed. Women who choose to be full-time mothers must have the assurance that their sacrifice of current and potential future earnings will be honored, and that women's and children's financial futures will be protected.

Stopping the Day Care Drip

On a policy level, the discussion of child care is dominated by questions of how to facilitate group day care. For example, one researcher wrote that "one objective of the Family Support Act of 1988 is to facilitate labor force entry of women with young children by improving their wages and reducing their child care costs."[12] Isn't there an illogic to having the words "facilitating the labor force entry of women with young children" in legislation bearing the title Family Support Act?

The majority of women report they're working at jobs because of economic need. And yet the feminist movement is being driven by "fulfillment" talk and arguments about women's careers being limited by the glass ceiling. As a result, the primary response to economic need has been to support women in the workplace, rather than to support them in making arrangements to work at home, where they can care for their children.

And frankly, the economics of this issue just don't make sense. The poorest women, those with an annual family income of less than $15,000 (which is 62 percent of all women in the labor force), spend an average of 24.8 percent of their income on child care.[13]

Let's sketch a financial portrait of this typical mother in the middle. Her income is $15,000 (remember, this is the upper end for the majority of women). Let's assume her husband also makes somewhere between $15,000 to $20,000.

At that income, in 1996, married filing jointly with one child, she would be allowed the standard federal income tax deduction of $6,750 and three personal exemptions at $2,550 each. Their total deductions would be $14,400, which puts them over the tax threshold. As a result, all of her earnings would add to their taxable income.

That means that every dollar she earns is taxed at 15 percent. The increase in their joint taxes, then, would be $2,250. She would also receive a child care tax credit of approximately $500, which would reduce her tax bill to $1,750. However, she would also have to pay FICA taxes, which at 7.65 percent would total $1,148. Her total tax bill comes to $2,898.

That leaves her $12,102. In order to get to work, she has to have transportation. Let's use a conservative $4 a day round-trip for bus or metro, and that totals $1,000 a year (fifty weeks). After taxes and transportation, she only has left $11,102.

We will estimate her child care expenses at $75 a week (that's what the average woman making $15,000 per year pays). For a year, that totals $3,750.[14]

That leaves this mother in the middle with net take-home earnings (earnings minus taxes minus transportation minus child care) of only $7,352. She's actually spending a third of her take-home income on child care. More importantly, she is only taking home 49 percent of her income. Over half of her earnings are gobbled up just in the expenses of working in the first place! And this simplistic analysis doesn't take into account any of the many other extra expenses incurred in entering the labor force.

This percentage of income spent on child care, of course, declines up the income scale, until women in the top class, those making over $50,000 and paying more than double what lower-income women do on child care, spend only 6.2 percent of their income.[15]

However, it is important to note that the majority of low-income women, 58 percent, do not purchase child care for their preschoolers; this contrasts with 70 percent of high-income women.[16]

The mother in the middle is spending a third of her take-home income on child care and ending up with less than $8,000 a year for other living expenses.

We need to reframe the issue.

The public policy discussion should be refocused on how to support women in combining their work with caring for children—how to craft the workplace of the twenty-first century with the aid of the Technological Revolution. Where the issue is economic need, we must focus on ways to assist mothers in generating income. Instead, today we focus on how to help women be the ideal worker—or over-worker—that too many businesses demand. Why are we helping women become the ideal workers that business wants them to be, rather than assisting women in becoming the quantity-time mothers that they want to be?

Tyrannosaurus Tax

The tax burden on American families has been increasing: in 1948, taxes on a median-income family of four were just 2 percent of their annual income. Today the tax burden on median income is 28 percent—fourteen times higher than fifty years ago.[17] Can it be a coincidence that as taxes have increased—leaving families with less disposable income—wives have felt greater economic pressure to work?

212 Mother in the Middle

The second tax element is the Dependent Care Tax Credit (DCTC). The largest of the federal programs involved in child care, the DCTC was budgeted at $2.5 billion for 1993.[18] However, in order to qualify for the DCTC, you must "incur the care expenses in order to earn income." For married couples, "this requires both spouses to work either at full- or part-time positions."[19] This policy not only discriminates against at-home mothers but also widens the economic gap between two-income and single-income families.

The Law of Unintended Consequences

Our tax policy is clearly skewed toward labor force participation for mothers. Child care subsidies work the same way. Not only do they encourage out-of-home care through the actual subsidies but they institutionalize child care, by the establishment of a federal child care bureaucracy. By the cash assistance the government gives, it further promotes usage of day care centers.

This is particularly noteworthy, given the evidence (addressed in chapter 8) that the majority of families have chosen relative care instead of institutionalized day care. But a mother and her relative who want to work together in providing care for a child in order to take advantage of the earmarked federal subsidies must overcome bureaucratic hurdles. For instance, to receive moneys from the Child Care and Development Block Grant, recipients "must meet applicable state and local standards or, if not regulated, be registered (including relatives)."[20]

Neither of these public policies—the tax credit or the federal child care subsidies—do anything for the mother who chooses to leave the workforce. It appears, then, that our current federal policies are designed in such a way as to provide assistance only to the mother who chooses to enter the labor force and place her child in some sort of paid child care arrangement. This is a tilting of the federal scales toward out-of-home, bureaucratic solutions.

Pro-Child Family Tax Reform

Fortunately, tax reform has now become a hot political issue. But this is all the more reason to pressure lawmakers to make certain that tax reform is family friendly.

With the flat tax coming into more serious consideration, the tax debate may change drastically. However, under our current tax system, the proposal to provide a per-child tax credit of some amount is certainly a step in the right direction. This has the advantage of providing all parents with assistance in the care of their children, to be used however each family most needs, which is more evenhanded than targeting a specific child-rearing cost, like child care, that not all parents incur.

An even more basic tax reform would be the elimination of the "marriage penalty" in the tax code. Currently, the standard deduction for a married couple is less than double that of a single person. We should remove the anti-marriage bias and make the married couple deduction at least double that of a single person. We should also increase the deduction for children as well.

If assisting parents with child care expenses (in home or not) is the goal, then we could target an increased deduction to parents of children under the age of five. Their taxes, after all, are subsidizing the public education of other taxpayers' older children. Or alternatively, we could eliminate the income-producing requirement of the Dependent Care Tax Credit and simply make it available to all families with children under five, with appropriate income restrictions.

Welfare Policy

Lastly, a troubling development in public policy has been the turn that welfare reform has taken. As the debate has progressed, it has increasingly centered on moving people off Aid to Families with Dependent Children (AFDC) and into jobs. While economic self-reliance is a laudable goal, the debate has largely ignored the fact that the majority of AFDC recipients are unmarried mothers with preschool-age children. While AFDC was originally established in the depression years to provide temporary assistance for the widow and orphan, it has evolved over the years to be a support program for mothers with "no marriage tie."

Certainly there is a need for reform. Two reform proposals under consideration, the benefit cap and time limits on benefits, are aimed at removing any economic incentive for a woman to have additional children while on welfare and at making public assistance a temporary condition. While these are important elements of the reform discussion, the real focus needs to be on encouraging and supporting family formation. What is accomplished by the proposal to require mothers of infants to work? Do we gain as much as the children lose?

Even some conservatives, who traditionally support mothers at home, are ignoring the larger societal ramifications of requiring AFDC moms to work. The tough "change welfare to workfare" rhetoric plays well. But won't it place some disadvantaged preschool children at an even greater disadvantage to reduce their contact with the one parent they do have and replace that parent with a "mother substitute"? This isn't "pro-family" strategy.

These questions were not lost on columnist Ellen Goodman, who wrote in 1995:

> In a world of working mothers, we have arrived at the point where there is virtually no public support for AFDC. Indeed, the women struggling hardest at the lowest-paying jobs are often the most angry at paying taxes for others to stay home. This anger is the real "mommy war" in America. . . .
>
> The message about what constitutes good motherhood circa 1995 is clear. This summer, Massachusetts Governor Bill Weld, waxing poetic about welfare reform, talked about the proud look in a child's eyes when his mother went off to her first job.

Was that child fifteen or two? Does it still matter? . . .
We have come through a great change of mind about
mothering. And yet we still haven't answered the
question asked at the onset: "Who will take care of
the children?"[21]

Who will take care of the children? Someone does have to
do it. In discussions of child care, the child development literature often refers to the "mother substitute." A mother's care
for her own child is always the standard. As a matter of public
policy, we should encourage what is best for the children. Why
should we settle for—much less promote—a substitute?

Moving to Higher Ground

Our search for peace must involve all facets of society—
the family, the community, businesses, and public policy. But it
starts with the individual mother.

The encouraging news is that we believe the revaluing of
motherhood is a work already in progress. While we heard,
from many mothers, of discouraging attacks and subtle put-
downs, there were many inspiring stories of moms fighting
back. And they are fighting back where it really counts: within
themselves.

Kirsten once took her first baby back to a reunion at her
college. "I thought it would be fun to show off the baby and
visit with these people," she said. Instead, one man commented
to her, "I can't believe you are wasting your four years of college education by staying home to take care of this baby."

"I was totally shocked," Kirsten told us. "I remember thinking, *Who do you want to raise the children of America, unedu-
cated people?*" Kirsten is now thirty and has four boys—not the
stereotypical, self-absorbed Generation X'er the media would
like to portray.

At the heart of the issue for mothers in the middle is the feminine identity crisis. So that's where we have to start—with women themselves becoming confident of their own unique gifts and abilities.

———————————

One truly remarkable mother of seven we talked to, Rebecca, said:

"I have just refused to get involved with the mommy wars. There are certain women who don't respond well to stay-at-home moms, and I suppose there are times when I could feel isolated by that, but I haven't worried about the people who are critical or who are making judgments about me."

Rebecca is secure in herself and in the choices she has made.

She, like the many mothers in the middle whose stories, wisdom, and practical strategies we will hear about in the next chapter, has found personal peace. And she's embraced the higher vision of motherhood we'll talk about in chapter 12.

Eleven

Finding Personal Peace: Where Should We Go?

Maybe we women remain better able to make decisions based on the voice that speaks from the heart and not that great, inchoate "they" out there that dictates career paths and life goals based on a cookie-cutter view of success and a disdain for personal happiness as an end in itself.

Anna Quindlen[1]

We (Charmaine and Deborah) know from personal experience what it feels like to be a mother in the middle. And as we said in chapter 1, if we have learned anything from our own lives, we have learned that there is not just one true path to ultimate motherhood. Different women can, and should, make different choices.

However, we also know that our choices as individual women and mothers have consequences—not only for us but for our families. Which is why, in this book, we are searching and calling for more and better choices for women—choices that meet the needs of our children by including, allowing for, and encouraging motherhood.

You may have finished reading the changes and choices proposed in chapter 10 and thought, *That's all well and good. Maybe motherhood could be better and easier in the future. But*

217

what about me? What about my family situation? And what about my children? I'm just one mother in the middle; how can I find peace for myself today?

This chapter is for you. Here we're going to hear from many of the mothers we talked to who have found balance in their lives. Mothers who have used their personal power to reach a higher ground and create a life of meaning and fulfillment for themselves, without leaving their children behind.

In their stories and quotes, we found hope and encouragement. And some general guidelines for reaching a personal peace, a sense of balance in the middle. From their experiences, we hope you can find strategies and words of wisdom you can apply to your life and your needs as a mother in the middle.

A Vision for Motherhood

Some of the mothers to whom we talked told us, "I am in the ideal situation" . . . "I'm really happy with my life right now" . . . "Life is working really well for us right now" . . . "Right now I'm doing what I want to be doing."

The voices of these same mothers were also saying, "No one can be a mother to my children but me—anyone can fill those other jobs" . . . "I consider putting loving, caring, responsible adults into our world to be a greater accomplishment than anything I could ever do as a high-powered executive of a major company" . . . "Success is knowing I've done the best I could, that my kids have turned out well" . . . "I felt that staying home with my children would be best for them. But after having children, I feel that it is really best for me as well."

And they were saying:

- "If I don't do anything else with my life, I will be satisfied, as an old woman, to look at my children and see two reasonably happy, content, well-adjusted adults."
- "We mothers have a lot of options open to us."
- "I know that when my children are older, if I so desire, I can return to the academic scene."

- "I feel confident that after ten years of mothering, I can go back when I want to and make it on the career track."
- "I can do other things. But I don't want to do them right now. I want to wait until the children are older."
- "I have not found it to be true that you cannot take a break from your career. You can go back after taking a break. You just may have to wait a little longer to be head of the company."

The mothers who were happiest with motherhood were women who had a vision for the significance of their roles in the lives of their children. They considered their work as mothers to be "my greatest work" and "the most important thing I will ever do."

These mothers also understood how short a time their children would be young. They chose to look at the long-term picture and sometimes forego short-term gain.

Their vision of motherhood gave them the strength to survive the diapers, the laundry, the isolation, the financial hardships. This sense of mission motivated them to build their support systems, to rearrange their priorities, to find creative solutions to financial problems, and to focus on the joys of children.

This overarching theme—this lofty vision of their role—permeated the stories of the women who felt that they had found balance in the higher middle ground of motherhood. But they arrived at that point by different routes.

So the rest of this chapter lays out some of the recurring strategies these mothers in the middle have followed, some of the well-worn paths that have led many women to their own personal peace.

Stepping Off the Fast Track

We talked to a number of on-the-rise, high-flying career women who made what was the painfully difficult decision to ground their careers—at least temporarily—in order to ease the pressures on their families and on themselves as mothers in the middle. These were women who described themselves as "driven," "a workhorse," and "a type-A personality."

One of these was Sylvia, the Madison Avenue executive you've already met (in chapters 3 and 10) who reached the breaking point after "working herself to the bone" trying to give 110 percent as a wife, a mother, and an "A+ player" at work. She finally decided the job had to give, because "I knew my children would never be children again." She went on to say:

"Other women in my company, women who were doing fine with their professional careers, pulled me aside and said, with a tinge of regret in their voices, 'If I could, I would do what you are doing.'

"And I talked to other women who entered the professional arena later in life, or who had returned to the workforce later after raising their kids. Their philosophy is that you can have it all—you just can't have it all at once. I liked that philosophy. That they took the time to raise their children and they have wonderful kids—that says something to me.

"I loved my job and it was tough to leave. But work will always be out there.

"I don't know what I'll do down the road. It is very much an unknown. Next year my oldest will be entering kindergarten. I know I will find a way to get involved at school. I keep an open mind for opportunities.

"Right now my focus is on the family, and that's really where it needs to be.

"I used to view the stay-at-home moms as, *Gosh, they have it so easy.* That was before I became one. Now, with three preschool children, I have never worked harder in my life!

"I miss the support I had at work, the adulation. The mental stimulation and the adult interaction on a day-to-day basis—I still miss that dreadfully. I don't want to complain, though. I have healthy children. I have a wonderful marriage with my husband. I have it pretty darn good.

"I look at all the bright-eyed, eager young women coming out of colleges and MBA programs today. Like my youngest sister. Someone needs to be telling them—and I really would like this message to get out: It is a myth that you can have it all. I'm absolutely convinced of it. And that's not conceding defeat; it's called getting real, people."

In the fall of 1994, when Pulitzer Prize–winning columnist Anna Quindlen, viewed for years by many women as the ultimate fast-track role model, announced her resignation as a regular contributor to the editorial pages of the *New York Times,* her reading public reacted with a fascinating mixture of disappointment, dismay, and disapproval. Many observers felt that this noted spokesperson for feminism was letting down the sisterhood of women by giving up such a powerful and influential position. Despite the fact that a major motivation behind the decision was her desire to devote more time to writing fiction, some liberals lamented their loss of an influential career woman to the lure and responsibilities of motherhood. At the same time, one conservative critic claimed that her decision showed women had no business in the workplace to begin with. Reflecting on the public uproar her very personal decision triggered, Quindlen wrote a December 1995 article for *Working Woman* magazine entitled, "Why I Quit." In it she talks about the challenge of juggling three full-time careers—writer for the *Times,* freelance novelist, and mother of three grade-school-age children. She recalls:

> I was so ambitious I once told a magazine writer that I intended to be childless all my life because I didn't want to trip over any little feet on my way to the top.
>
> I am almost as incredulous, looking back at that young woman, as are many of those observing her, in

middle age, deciding to take a less spectacular path. To that extent my children were indeed behind this decision, as they have been behind literally every decision about the broad parameters of my life I have made since the eldest was born a dozen years ago. They have given me perspective on the pursuit of joy and the passage of time. I miss too much when I am out of their orbit, and as they grow, like a time-lapse photograph that makes a flower out of a bud in scant minutes, I understand that I will have time to pursue a more frantic agenda when they have gone on to pursue their own. But they have made a more frantic agenda seem somehow less seductive than a satisfying one.[2]

Sequencing: The Art of Taking One Thing at a Time

Shannon has a teaching degree and taught school until she was pregnant with her first child. After his birth, she stayed home full-time for six years. During those at-home years, she became a La Leche League leader, organized a mother's support and education group, worked as a volunteer with an in-hospital infant program, and had another son.

The year her second son was two and her older son began school, Shannon went back to work. But she taught at a two-day preschool program that allowed her young son to go with her to work. By working only two days, she could volunteer at the school, as room mother, and one year as PTA president. After her youngest started kindergarten, she substitute-taught two or three days a week at her sons' school, for two years. Then she took a full-time job at a pet store.

Shannon returned to full-time employment, in part for the income and "partly to have something to do." Now she combines her teaching with her animal expertise. She not only conducts educational field trips around the pet store but she also takes animals to local schools for educational demonstrations.

These activities were her special projects and have raised the visibility of the pet store in the community.

She works a few hours every Saturday, in exchange for having every Wednesday off. That enables her to continue to volunteer at the boys' school and stay active in that part of their lives.

"I feel successful right now," she said. "At some point along the line, I would like to see my kids as responsible members of the community. Have them graduate from college and have good jobs. Not just not be in the troupe but be good, contributing members of the community. That would be real success."

A number of the mothers we talked to who felt successful as mothers followed Shannon's pattern. Like Sylvia, they have come to the conclusion that women can't have it all, at least not all at once.

Arlene Rossen Cardozo called this pattern "sequencing" in her book by the same name.[3] Many mothers we interviewed tailored sequencing in different ways to fit their own needs. But most took a few years completely off from paid employment to focus on young children. Then as their children got older, they added volunteer activities and/or part-time employment. Some mothers rejoined the workforce in the same field, but many of the mothers we talked to found their careers taking interesting turns, in different directions, after motherhood.

Volunteer Work: Filling the Holes in Society

Erica is the mother of three. Her husband is a graduate student. Although their finances are tight, both are committed to Erica staying at home with the children. But being an at-home mother certainly doesn't mean she is always at home.

Two years ago she began to do volunteer work at a local food bank. Needy families who come there receive staples, either free or for pennies on the dollar.

224 Mother in the Middle

Before long, Erica became the principal buyer. Each week, she takes an old, unheated van and drives to a warehouse in a nearby city, a half-hour drive each way. At the warehouse, she carefully chooses the best buys, trying to make the most of the food bank's limited financial resources. She then loads the van with her purchases and returns to her town, where she unloads the food. She usually has help putting it up on the shelves.

"My children make sacrifices to allow me to make the weekly trip," Erica told us. "Many times they help out. My ten-year-old understands the impact of our effort and hopefully is internalizing these values that we put forth as a family."

Almost all the mothers who got off the fast track and are sequencing told us about doing volunteer work. We talked to mothers who helped out with schools, PTA, churches, food banks, homeless shelters, La Leche League, United Way, Meals on Wheels, Habitat for Humanity, teen pregnancy programs, hospital child-life programs. All of these, plus many more community and service organizations, rely on volunteer help.

These mother-volunteers we talked with have learned that life's scorecard is not a paycheck. That unpaid volunteer work is real work, valuable work that enriches their lives, the lives of their families, and the life of the community around them, work that can and should be included in their resumes, if and when they want to return to paid employment.

You Don't Have to Be a Professor to Take a Sabbatical

Danielle worked in retail for six years before having children. Her husband has a middle-management job for a manufacturing company. Danielle told us:

"I've played with the idea of going back to college and becoming an accountant. Maybe when the boys get older, I will do that. I do some volunteer things at the school, going on field trips and reading to their classes. I get a lot of fulfillment out of that.

"But one of the joys of being an at-home mom, for me, is having time to spend with my grandmother.

"I have always been interested in genealogy. When I was working full-time, there just wasn't time to get into that. But early on I decided that if I was going to be at home with children, I wanted to pursue that interest.

"When the boys were small, I found time every week or so to go to the library or to visit local cemeteries to look for family gravestones. And I started going to my grandmother's house every Thursday morning. We would visit and I'd tell her how I was doing on my genealogy research. She would answer my questions about the family tree and then tell me and the boys stories about her younger days.

"The boys are in school now. But I would never give up my Thursday mornings with my grandmother. I don't let anything else interfere with that, except when the boys are sick.

"When our family gets together, everyone wants to know what new things I have learned about our family heritage. Three or four years ago my husband and I bought a family computer and I started keeping my genealogical records on disk. Now, before big family gatherings, I'll print out my latest information and make copies for aunts and uncles and cousins.

"A year or so ago I started writing out some of my grandmother's stories. I'm hoping to compile a collection of them and maybe even have them published. That work is really satisfying to me.

"My life right now is my family, and I'm really happy with my life."

Some of the voices we heard were from mothers who, like Danielle, had used their years at home with children to enrich their lives by learning or studying. Some mothers took night classes; others attended seminars and workshops in order to pursue an interest that enriched themselves but for which they had never before had time.

Home-Based Business

Esther has three children. Her husband is a minister, a dynamic preacher who is often asked to speak at other churches. The year their third child was born, Esther decided to ease their finances by starting a business out of their home. She audiotaped her husband's Sunday sermons and marketed them to other preachers and churches, through a mail-order business.

The first year, her business grossed over one hundred thousand dollars.

Esther told us:

"Money-wise it was a fabulous year, but work-wise it just about physically killed me. I had a new baby and I was nursing her. I took care of three preschool children twenty-four hours a day, seven days a week, ran the business, and never took a break. A friend of mine looked me in the eye and said, 'You are the only person I know who has a full-time job and no child care.' I guess I thought that since I was 'at home,' I wasn't working!"

Esther cut back some on her workload and hired a baby-sitter for six hours a week.

"I work my tail off during that time. But that has made it easier to just kick back some the rest of the week and not feel panicked all the time. I like my business, because it is something tangible, a little more permanent. And I am helping out money-wise."

For several of the mothers we talked with, becoming a mother was the turning point that forced them to do something creative, something they never would have done otherwise. Motherhood launched them into new entrepreneurial careers.

Margaret didn't marry Robert until she was twenty-eight, and they didn't have children for another seven years. By then she had spent fifteen years as a fund-raiser for various non-profit organizations. After working that long as a professional, motherhood was a major life change. But she was ready to try something different.

"Frankly," she told us, "I'm so grateful I had children, because otherwise I wouldn't have gone into business for myself." Margaret now runs a catalog mail-order business out of her basement office. "For me, it's just such a high. To drive home from a meeting with my distributor and know that we sold out of a particular item—that is really, really exciting to me. Speaking of rushes, that's a pretty good one. It's a lot of fun. It's worth making the juggle of everything I have to juggle to make it happen."

It is a juggle, and Margaret admits that there aren't enough hours in the day. But the choices she has made allow her to be with her children and still grow professionally. She fits all of her work into four mornings a week, during which time she has a baby-sitter.

Millie is a mom who has lived on both sides of the mommy wars. She was an architect who took a three-month maternity leave after the birth of her son and only took five weeks off after the birth of her daughter. She says the decision to stay home was "a long, protracted one." She raced back after her daughter was born to be sure her ideas were given enough weight in an ongoing project. "I always loved my job," she said. "I always felt that I really wanted to do that."

But as time went by, she began to burn out. Her husband was in a high-stress position, so she started to feel that everything at home was landing on her shoulders. She felt very unhappy. She told us, "I felt like, *This is not right. I'm cheating someone and I'm probably cheating everyone.* I just felt that I needed to be at home."

Nevertheless, she still felt she needed to be working at something. As a person who had always done creative and strategic work professionally, she needed an outlet. "I know that from the point of view of finding a sense of self-worth," she said, " I need work outside of my family. My whole world cannot be successfully reduced to just taking care of my children. I know I need to do something, and I'm trying to find that middle ground."

She found several things. Shortly before the birth of their third child, they moved to another city, and the two changes— quitting her job and moving to a new town—forced her into creative action. She has started a home-based business designing and marketing greeting cards and has also become a published writer.

She has become very creative in getting her work done. "I tell the kids, 'OK now, let's all go to work. I'll get your paper and pencils out, and I'll get on my computer.' They think that's great. . . . We have a little table close by where they sit and work while I'm working, and we all work together."

Not everyone has the personality or the sales experience to market a hundred thousand dollar's worth of sermon tapes in one year, or the wherewithal to launch a mail-order business or create a line of greeting cards. But many mothers have found ways to earn money from their homes, work that was flexible and could be fit in and around the schedules of their children.

Some mothers did home day care. One mother sold Amway products; another had a home-decorating business that consisted of ordering wallpaper and sewing drapes, lampshades, and other accessories to match. We talked to former teachers who manned homework hot lines for the local school system or tutored students weekends and evenings.

The Part-Time Solution

Before children, Courtney worked at a job that required sixty to eighty hours a week. When she and her husband decided they were ready for children, Courtney went back to school to get a license as a veterinary technician so that she would have a part-time career. She explained, "I knew I wanted to be able to raise our children and not have somebody else do it."

She works at a veterinary clinic two days a week, an average of sixteen hours per week. Courtney's mom takes care of the baby. She made it clear to Courtney that two days was her limit. She wanted to be Grandma, not Mom, to the baby.

About her work situation, Courtney told us:

"Sometimes, if they need me, I'll put in extra hours. They're very flexible. They know my family comes first. The times I've had to take off for emergency leave, they are very good about that.

"I'm happy being home to see my son develop and do new things. When he's learning and I know I'm responsible for at least some part of that—it makes me feel good.

"In my job I've learned so much, and it helps me to have an outlet—to be something other than a mom. I get to have that little outlet of adulthood, and it makes me appreciate being home with him even more."

Courtney loves the at-home-mom–part-time job combination. "I have the best of both worlds—being able to do both," she said.

Tag Team Match

Gwen feels much the same way about the tag team strategy she and her husband have worked out. She works evenings at a gift shop and arranges her schedule so that three-year-old Ivey is in day care only two hours before Gwen's husband picks their daughter up on his way home from work. Gwen told us:

"My husband is having to work hard and has to help more at home. But he likes for me to bring in some money, and he likes the changes in me. He thinks that it's good for me to work. That I'm a happier, more self-confident person with a job. I think I do feel better about myself.

"Our oldest daughter (who's ten) is gifted. So we are considering putting her in a private school to help her reach her potential. If I work, we will be able to pay for that. That feels good to me.

"I think any conflict I feel is mostly within myself—my personal struggle: what I should do versus what I want to do. I've recently been asked to consider taking a daytime job as store manager. I enjoy my job and I enjoy the paycheck. But right now I also want to be home with my kids and be as involved in their lives as I can be."

Finding a Support Group: Mothers Need Mothers

Glenda had worked in a large city. When she married, she and her husband moved to a town near his work, sixty miles from her office, and she commuted for several years. Then she left her career to be at home with her daughter. She told us:

"The first year after our daughter was born was very difficult for me. Until the baby arrived, I was never around home enough to put my roots down and develop friendships.

"All my friends were working women, from my office. They told me I was crazy. That I would be miserable and I would hate my life. They told me I was making the worst decision of my life.

"I knew I was doing the right thing for me. But I felt very pulled.

"My mother was supportive. But my dad felt that I had worked real hard and gone to school, that I'd had this goal and I had quit. I never felt support from him. He thought I was wasting my life. That hurt.

"I have a wonderful support group now. But that took several years to manage. I was the first one in this community and in my church to quit my job and come home with my kids."

Glenda became involved with La Leche League and met other breast-feeding mothers who were at home with their children. And she organized a mother's support group at her church. She arranged speakers, even when only four or five mothers were coming. Now a group of twelve mothers regularly meet. Some work part-time, some are at-home moms, and one has a business in her home. Glenda continued:

"We all have children about the same age, and we are the same ages and have the same interests. We do Bible study together, we pray for each other. I had surgery last week, and they all brought me food.

"It is wonderful to have a group of friends like I have."

A great majority of the happiest, most contented mothers we talked to had found ways to connect with other moms on a regular basis. Some found support through their churches, others through La Leche League, others through mother-oriented groups like MOPS and MotherCare. But all considered support from other mothers in the middle to be essential to their survival.

Husband Support: We Can't Do It by Ourselves

Eva is an at-home mom with three preschool children. Her family's life is complicated by the fact that her husband, Tom, works at a job that isn't all he wants it to be. But he's convinced it is important for their children's welfare for Eva to be at home with them.

In order to ease their family's life, Tom took a job on the second shift.

At first Eva worried about having him gone at bedtime. But she soon realized that his schedule had many advantages:

"I've got it pretty good the way things are right now. When my husband is gone, half of his work hours are when the children are sleeping. I have to keep the kids quiet first thing in the morning, but he's up usually about 10:00 a.m. His first waking hours of the day, when he's fresh, he's here with me and the kids. So we do more family things while the kids are awake.

"Back when he was working a regular shift, he did a lot of overtime. He would get home at 7:30 p.m.—only an hour before the kids would head to bed. They'd be tired; we'd have a late supper, but nobody felt like doing anything. This way, everybody is awake and energetic, and we have several hours in the middle of the day to be together. Sometimes it's nice just having him be here while I clean up the house.

"I'm lucky: my husband is an important part of my support system."

Husband support seems to be an integral part of the lives of mothers who feel successful. We heard mothers say:

- "My husband has always made me feel very important to be doing what I'm doing. It's impossible for me to see how any woman could make the choice to be home without that kind of support."
- "My husband's role? I couldn't do what I do without him. If he were not supportive, it wouldn't happen."
- "He takes the financial burden, because he knows what I do for the kids is important."
- "Since children, my husband's perspective has changed, too. Instead of being the best engineer, he wants to be the best Barbie dresser in the world—next to his daughters, of course. Without his support, I couldn't do what I do."

A heartening number of the woman we talked to only confirmed our (Charmaine and Deborah's) beliefs: that raising children is a team operation and that marriage, rightly viewed, is a partnership of equals. In a partnership, as a team pulling together toward common goals, all parts of the whole are valued for their unique contributions. Having a healthy marriage in which both people understand that they are working together is probably one of the most important elements of happy motherhood.

Mothers may have lost the psychic income of being on a team in their workplace, but they can rebuild that sense of working toward a shared vision, within their family. It's in that context that a mother's sacrifices for her children make sense.

Time after time we found ourselves talking to a happy mother (not without struggles, but content), who would volunteer that the most important thing was that her husband is supportive.

Rebecca told us that when things got tight for them financially, her first reaction was to go to work. But her husband, Alan, supported her in staying home. "He's always the one to remind me of why I'm doing what I'm doing," she said. "If he had ever wavered on that at all, I'd probably have been out the door with a job. But he has never wavered. . . . He's always made me feel very important to be doing what I'm doing."

Admittedly, some husbands had to be convinced.

"At first my husband was very skeptical about how we were going to make it," one mother told us. "Now we take one day at a time and quit worrying about everything else. He's really come a long way. He wants me to be at home, and he's really glad that I am. He sees the value of what I am doing."

Another women said, "My husband wanted me to return to work after one or two years. He worries about money, and I know he would like to have more things. But the pressure has faded in time. Now he lets me know that he appreciates what I'm doing with the babies."

The Road Less Traveled

At some point in the forgotten past of some American literature class, most of us probably read the classic Robert Frost poem "The Road Not Taken." When we remember it today, we see new and special meaning in the words as they relate to mothers in the middle.

The Road Not Taken

Two Roads diverged in a yellow wood,
And sorry I could not travel both
And be one traveler, long I stood
And looked down one as far as I could
To where it bent in the undergrowth;
Then took the other, as just as fair,
And having perhaps the better claim,
Because it was grassy and wanted wear;
Though, as for that, the passing there
Had worn them really about the same,
And both that morning equally lay
In leaves no steps had trodden black.
O I kept the first for another day!
Yet knowing how way leads on to way,
I doubted if I should ever come back.
I shall be telling this with a sigh
Somewhere ages and ages hence:
Two roads diverged in a wood, and I—
I took the one less traveled by,
And that has made all the difference.[4]

We all make choices that set us moving down a particular path in life. And some of those choices we can never make again. We cannot return to being twenty-two years old and deciding on our first career. Many times when we make a life choice, we are, in effect, forever closing doors on other possibilities.

And yet although that principle applies to many situations, it does not apply to all. Life is more flexible than many mothers seem to view it. Many women and men change careers at some point in their lives. They reexamine their priorities and interests and look back to the roads not taken in their lives. Especially today, with colleges and universities welcoming older students and with the Technological Revolution making home computers and electronic commuting commonplace, our generation has unprecedented freedom to change the focus and direction of our lives, to choose again some path we did not take earlier in our lives.

Like Shannon, who used her first career in teaching to enrich her second career of working in the pet store, some mothers reenter the workforce in a different capacity. We talked to mothers who had been teachers or nurses, who took several years off and returned to be better teachers and nurses. Other mothers decided they could postpone their dreams for a time. One woman told us, "I decided I could wait until I'm forty-five or fifty, after my children are in school, to earn my Pulitzer."

We talked to other, employed mothers who said that they would love to spend more time with their children but that: their boss needs them; they want to earn money now and be able to retire early; they are afraid a job will not be there when they want to return to the workforce; their husbands wanted them to work; or they just figured that going back to work was "what women did today."

Yet the mothers who had taken time to focus their lives around motherhood told us that choice had enriched their lives. These mothers had not found their motherhood to have limited their possibilities for their future. Rather, they found motherhood had broadened and extended their vision.

These mothers told us over and over again, "My children will only be young for a short time, and I want to be there when they need me."

The children who are now crying, "Look at me!" will, before we know it, be graduating from high school and moving away from home. Now is the one time of our lives for us to be crazy about our kids.

It's encouraging that more and more women seem to be discovering this truth for themselves. Indeed, feminist free-lance writer Barbara Ehrenreich, noting the trend in a recent *Working Mother* article entitled "In Search of a Simpler Life," concluded:

> Meaningful work and a balanced life are deep-rooted and genuine human needs. Like any needs, they can be repressed or ignored for years at a time, but sooner or later they're going to assert themselves. Women aren't downshifting in greater numbers than men simply because women tend to have greater responsibility for children, but because child-raising provides us with a built-in standard for meaningful work. Not many jobs—paying jobs, that is—are as innately gratifying and purposeful as helping a tiny person evolve into a full-grown human. But you don't have to be a mother, or even a female, to wonder how your life is going to look from your deathbed: like a maze littered with scraps of old spreadsheets and credit card bills, or like a path that actually led some-where?[5]

Life is short. But childhood is shorter. And motherhood is the one road, if not taken, to which we can never return.

Twelve

Restoring Real
Feminine Power

*What happens at your house is more important
than what happens at the White House.*

Barbara Bush to the
Wellesley College graduates, 1992[1]

As we finished talking with Victoria, the first of the "voices
we have heard" mothers you met as we began this book,
she told us that supervising ten thousand employees doesn't
compare to mothering two small children:

"If I could wish for one thing, I would turn the clock back
to where we put ourselves on this perpetual cycle where I
became the driving career force. What I would have done is,
when I had my children, I would have stayed at home. I would
have been there primarily for them during these years of their
lives, and then I would have pursued the full-time career after
I'm no longer the major influence on the children's lives. So if
I could turn the clock back, I'd do some things differently and
delay the whole career process."

Like many professional women, Victoria was afraid. Afraid
that if she stepped off the fast track, she would never manage

to climb back on. A few years farther down the road now, life looks a lot different. "Now, having seen my life's course in front of me," she commented, "knowing what I know today—I would be willing to risk it. "

Maybe one of the reasons she felt that fear was that like many of us, she had absorbed society's devaluing messages about motherhood. We asked her, as we asked many of the women we talked to, whether or not she felt that women, and particularly mothers, were powerful.

Victoria's answer was simple and straightforward. "No," she said, "I don't feel mothers are powerful."

What is power, anyway? For years, feminists have been bitterly decrying the fact that power is consolidated in the hands of white men. Think, for instance, of the political arena: from *Ms.* magazine and NOW and other feminist groups, we regularly hear how terrible it is that the majority of our elected representatives are men. Then there is the glass ceiling: we are constantly told that it is a travesty that mostly men rule the boardrooms. Naturally, this means, as night follows day, that men have all the *power*.

Or do they?

A higher vision of motherhood demands a recognition and appreciation of intrinsic feminine power. All of us, men and women, have power in the unique gifts and abilities we as individuals have that give us opportunities to affect people and change the world around us. That kind of power is limited only by our own vision.

But in addition to that, mothers have a specific—and unparalleled—power in the opportunity for influence we hold through our guidance of the next generation. That is a fundamental truth of life that the feminine mystake seems to have obliterated for our generation.

Men simply do not have all the power. In many ways, we as women have access to power that far exceeds the political and business strength men have.

It's a Woman's World

The fifties may not have been perfect, but there was an understanding that women were powerful. Witness the 1954 movie *A Woman's World*, starring Lauren Bacall. Three businessmen are vying for a spectacular promotion. The president of the company can't decide between them, so he brings all three, with their wives, to company headquarters in New York City for a weekend to meet with them personally and make his decision.

The most fascinating moment in the movie is a conversation between Lauren Bacall's character and one of the other wives. Mrs. Talbott, the charming, scheming other wife, begins the conversation that gives the movie its title:

" . . . besides, I'm sure we both are aware that we happen to be living in a man's world . . ."

"You haven't any children, have you, Mrs. Talbott?" asks Bacall's character.

"No."

"You know, I think if you and Mr. Talbott had children, you might realize that a man like your husband would be working more for his children than for you. And you wouldn't mind that, because they would be your children, too, and you'd know you gave them to him. That's why, Mrs. Talbott, it isn't a man's world, it's a woman's world."[2]

Living in a post-feminist age, this seems a stunning statement. We are so unused to thinking in these terms—motherhood has been so devalued—that it takes a minute to process Bacall's point. It's startling because it seems so anachronistic.

But is it?

This insight from another age has been lost: women hold power through the awesome nature of their responsibility as mothers of the next generation. And they have power in the lives of the men to whom they have given an intimate connection to the future.

But even more important is the layered meaning beneath her surface point about feminine power. She is saying that working together as husbands and wives, mothers and fathers, each contributing in our own way as part of a team for the benefit of one's children, is the real power that makes the world go round. Sadly, this fundamental truth has been obscured. Because, really, it isn't a man's world or a woman's world—it's our world together.

Back to the Future

There was a time in our country when motherhood was a powerful institution. Let's go back for a moment to the fifties—the 1850s. Let's revisit the cult of womanhood that we mentioned in chapter 9.

Following the Revolutionary War, there was a recognition that mothers were needed to train citizens for the new democracy. As a result, motherhood gained in stature, and the movement to educate women gained ground. This appreciation for the importance of mothers grew and solidified until, by the early part of the nineteenth century, motherhood had become a deeply honored institution. As historian Glenna Matthews explains it:

> For the first time in American history, both home and woman's special nature were seen as uniquely valuable. . . . Wherever a middle-class housewife turned—whether to her minister's words from the pulpit or to her favorite reading matter—she could see and hear her value and the value of the home for which she was responsible being affirmed.[3]

It is precisely this cultural support for motherhood that has been destroyed. Historians often focus on the ways that the development of the "women's sphere" during this period was limiting for women. But often, in focusing on that element of the historical record, we miss the power these women did wield—and thereby miss possible lessons for us today.

By according so much status to motherhood, a connection between the private and public developed: women had societal influence—and power—far beyond their limited women's sphere.

If this is our model, motherhood needn't be limiting. Feminine power should be a vital force in the community, in the state, in the nation.

The quintessential example is a well-known nineteenth-century housewife, Harriet Beecher Stowe—a woman who, in the midst of raising seven children, helped change the world by writing *Uncle Tom's Cabin*. Many have heard that when Abraham Lincoln met her at the White House in 1862, he reportedly remarked, "So you're the little woman who wrote the book that started this great war!" But few know how firmly that book is embedded in Stowe's own experience of motherhood.

In the early summer of 1849, a cholera epidemic broke out in Cincinnati, near Walnut Hills, the Stowe home. By July her beloved baby Charley, who was a year and a half old, had become ill. Stowe's husband was away at the time, so she wrote to tell him the news:

> July 10. Yesterday little Charley was taken ill, not seriously, and at any other season I should not be alarmed. . . . I still think it best that you should not return.

> July 12. Yesterday I carried Charley to Dr. Pulte, who spoke in such a manner as discouraged and frightened me. . . . I came home with a heavy heart, sorrowing, desolate, and wishing my husband and father were here.

> July 15. Charley apparently recovering but still weak and feeble . . .

> July 23. At last, my dear, the hand of the Lord hath touched us. We have been watching all day by the dying bed of little Charley, who is gradually sinking.

About four days ago he was taken with decided cholera, and now there is no hope of his surviving this night. . . . I dare not trust myself to say more but shall write again soon.

July 26. My Dear Husband—At last it is over and our dear little one is gone from us. He is now among the blessed. My Charley—my beautiful, loving, gladsome baby, so loving, so sweet, so full of life and hope and strength—now lies shrouded, pale and cold, in the room below. Never was he anything to me but a comfort. He has been my pride and joy. Many a heartache has he cured for me. Many an anxious night have I held him to my bosom and felt the sorrow and loneliness pass out of me with the touch of his little warm hands. Yet I have just seen him in his death agony, looked on his imploring face when I could not help nor soothe nor do one thing, not one, to mitigate his cruel suffering, do nothing but pray in my anguish that he might die soon.[4]

In the next year, Congress passed the Fugitive Slave Law, which required northerners to assist in the capture and return of runaway slaves. Soon the North was full of tragic stories of captured fugitives. Stowe's sister, Isabella Beecher, wrote a letter from Boston in 1850 telling Harriet some of these stories, and in it she urged, "Now, Hattie, if I could use a pen as you can, I would write something that would make this whole nation feel what an accursed thing slavery is."[5]

Harriet, upon reading the letter, declared, "I will write something. I will if I live." Over the next two years, she did just that.

Uncle Tom's Cabin mobilized the sentiments of a nation against the horrors of slavery by making the suffering of slaves real for the readers. Stowe herself empathized most deeply with the slave mothers she heard of who were forcibly separated from their babies and children. The loss of a baby was suffering so deep that the anguish reached across entrenched racial lines. Stowe knew that anguish personally.

Many years later, in a letter explaining how she came to write *Uncle Tom's Cabin*, Stowe told how Charley's death motivated her:

> It was at his dying bed and at his grave that I learned what a poor slave mother may feel when her child is torn away from her. In those depths of sorrow which seemed to me immeasurable, it was my only prayer to God that such anguish might not be suffered in vain. . . . I felt that I could never be consoled for it, unless this crushing of my own heart might enable me to work out some great good to others. . . .
>
> I allude to this here because I have often felt that much that is in *[Uncle Tom's Cabin]* had its root in the awful scenes and bitter sorrows of that summer.[6]

This is the intrinsic power of motherhood. What Betty Friedan so casually dismissed as a sad, sick "love affair with their own children" connected Harriet Beecher Stowe, and connects every mother in the middle, to the universal joys and sorrows of life. But it's through that connection that we find a platform and the passion needed for making a difference in our world.

Glenna Matthews's historical analysis makes the same basic point—that the cult of womanhood assigned moral authority to the housewife and that this gave Harriet Beecher Stowe and her contemporaries a platform for speaking out against societal evils like slavery:

> The cult of domesticity was predicated in part on the idea that the home has an expressly political function. . . . The political impact of *Uncle Tom's Cabin*, filled as it is with domestic imagery, demonstrated how the influence of home on the world could manifest itself. . . . When the home acquired so diverse and

244 Mother in the Middle

expanded a set of roles in the early nineteenth century—political, religious, emotional, and social—it ceased to be automatically taken for granted by men. . . . Middle-class women began to organize for exerting influence in the world as never before and in such a way that public and private values were genuinely intermingled rather than being dichotomized.[7]

As we work to restore feminine power in our generation, this is a historical model that needs dusting off. Motherhood and home should still be a platform for action. And our children's future can still be a powerful motivator.

One mother told us that being a mother has fundamentally altered her convictions:

"I find that my passions have changed since having children. We just built a new library in [our town], and I was on the building committee. I was on that committee because I wanted something for the future of my children. I gave a lot of time for that. I do a lot of work with my church. I work with the teenage girls. Somebody pointed out to me that by working with teens, I'm setting the road for my own kids. I found the things that I'm very interested in are not necessarily one on one with my kids or their age group but with their future."

Are we arguing for a retreat from the public arena? Not in the least. We believe a higher vision will lead us to a . . .

Radical Motherhood

True feminine power should be focused on creating a culture that recognizes the importance of children and acknowledges the eternal significance of sacrificing some of our own ambitions on their behalf. That does not mean that motherhood should be limiting for women. Far from being an oppressor of women, it can be their liberation. We should challenge one another to see the new horizons that serving our children can open up.

Words like "sacrifice" and "service" can make our modern, individualistic hearts cringe. But why do we not recognize that anything worth having in life requires some kind of sacrifice? Isn't it hypocritical to argue, as many feminists do, that it's OK for a woman to make sacrifices for her career—but not for her own children?

The wonderful irony is that we talked with many women who found motherhood to be the most freeing experience of their lives. Even in the midst of the incredible constraints that being a mother brought to them, new opportunities for personal and professional growth opened up.

Indeed, our interviews have convinced us that we have too often confused service with servitude. There is a distinct difference: in servitude we are so diminished that we lose ourselves. And when mothers in the middle do that, it is a very real loss for everyone. Service produces growth: we serve from a position of internal strength—and in so doing, gain strength and experience the power and meaning of servanthood.

Finding Yourself

What is being radical all about?

We need to take charge of our own futures! Power isn't something given, like a royal knighthood—it must be seized. Feminist author Naomi Wolf has commented that women are naive about power: there aren't that many positions at the top beyond the glass ceiling. Why should the men sitting in those seats give them up willingly for women—or other men? [9] We are the daughters of the Daughters of Liberty, who helped throw the tea in the Boston Harbor. We are the daughters of the pioneer women who crossed the Rocky Mountains. That's our heritage as American women in this land of opportunity.

We don't need to have someone remove the glass ceiling for us. We've got better things to do.

Why are we still talking about employment as if that is our only source of fulfillment? Or day care as if that is what we want for our children? Survey after survey shows that it is not what moms today want. So why is day care near the top of the so-called women's agenda? That is decidedly not radical motherhood. Why not dare to fight for what we really want? Let us seize the day and bring our children up and out of the shadows.

In the Bible, we find this prototype of radical motherhood. King Solomon called her:

The Wife of Noble Character

Who can find a virtuous wife?
For her worth is far above rubies.
The heart of her husband safely trusts her;
So he will have no lack of gain.
She seeks wool and flax,
And willingly works with her hands.
She is like the merchant ships,
She brings her food from afar.
She also rises while it is yet night,
And provides food for her household,
And a portion for her maidservants.
She considers a field and buys it;
From her profits she plants a vineyard.
She girds herself with strength.
And strengthens her arms.
She perceives that her merchandise is good,
And her lamp does not go out by night.
She extends her hand to the poor,
Yes, she reaches out her hands to the needy.
She is not afraid of snow for her household,
For all her household is clothed with scarlet.

She makes tapestry for herself;
Her clothing is fine linen and purple.
Her husband is known in the gates,
When he sits among the elders of the land.
She makes linen garments and sells them,
And supplies sashes for the merchants.
Strength and honor are her clothing;
She shall rejoice in time to come.
She opens her mouth with wisdom,
And on her tongue is the law of kindness.
She watches over the ways of her household,
And does not eat the bread of idleness.
Her children rise up and call her blessed;
Her husband also, and he praises her.
"Many daughters have done well,
But you excel them all."
Charm is deceitful and beauty is vain,
But a woman who fears the Lord, she shall be
     praised.
Give her of the fruit of her hands,
And let her own works praise her in the gates.[8]
     (Emphasis ours.)

What does radical motherhood look like? It isn't super-mom. Radical motherhood is flagrantly making choices. Throwing the briefcase icon into the wind. It's scorched earth. Defiantly feminine. Maybe even . . . maternal. Psychologist, counselor, and author Brenda Hunter told us that "it isn't good for women to live in a constant state of struggle."

We need to carve out that personal peace. Rest for a while in childhood's challenge.

Radical motherhood is deciding with our heads to do the absolute best for our children and letting our hearts follow.

The mother in the middle, in her heart, wants to be a wise woman. Yes, she wants to be recognized professionally. But she wants her children to rise up and call her blessed.

"What do you need to feel successful?" we asked the many women we interviewed. The answer was in their children.

There are a lot of scorecards in life. But only one that really endures.

Marda Herz, a twenty-six-year-old physical therapy student, wants to someday be an at-home mom. "I grew up without a mom. . . . I don't want to see my children go through what we had to go through." Her mother, Fredda Herz Brown, psychologist and founder of family business consultants Metropolitan Group, says she "never felt any guilt about" pursuing her career while trying to raise two children.[9]

Ms. Brown made it to the top, but at what price? The story about her daughter's opinion of her mother appeared on the front page of the *Wall Street Journal*, the bible of the business world.

What a contrast to the wise woman of the Bible. She too is a businesswoman. An extraordinarily successful one—she has smashed the glass ceiling. In her day, being praised in the gates was a front-page *Wall Street Journal* equivalent. But her story reads entirely differently: her children rise up and call her blessed.

What lessons she has to teach us! No milquetoast saint, she. She is radical motherhood. Her life models so many important points: her husband supports her with praise; her household is interconnected to the community (she helps the poor); her work is focused on the well-being of her household (she watches over the ways of her household, and they are all clothed in scarlet); but she's not an ascetic—this is a woman who dresses beautifully (fine linen and purple were the cashmere of the day); and she received praise for her own works. She was even ahead of the power curve by thousands of years on the fitness craze—girding herself with strength and strengthening her arms!

There's no belittling this woman as just a housewife—she's our entrepreneurial model. She's into imports and exports and real estate transactions. In addition, it appears that she cooks, makes clothes, and has other creative outlets as well.

This is a powerful woman. This is radical motherhood.

In the end, it's not the fleeting kudos or arbitrary atta-boys that show enduring success. There is greater praise to be gained from those who know us best. The fully successful woman can succeed on many levels, but as she looks back on a whole life, what will matter most will be whether or not "her children rise up and call her blessed."

Closing Tribute—
Lives We Have Seen

We began this book with our own personal stories of motherhood, and "voices we have heard"—words of women struggling to cope as mothers in the middle. Throughout the book, we've included the wisdom and experiences of many more women we've met, known, or interviewed—women whose concerns and stories have helped direct and shape our thinking. Now, as we close, we want to recognize the two women who most shaped our lives by first modeling radical motherhood for us.

Charmaine's Tribute

Still to this day, the most soothing sound on earth for me is the tappity, tappity, tap of a typewriter. When I was a little girl, my mother, Janice Shaw Crouse, was hard at work on her doctorate in communication theory. But as she was the mother of two small children, progress was slow. Many, many nights, her studies didn't begin until my brother, Gil, and I were in bed. So I remember the secure, warm feeling of drifting off to sleep with the steady, rhythmic sound of my mother typing her papers late into the night.

My mother made it look so easy that it wasn't until I was an adult—and a mother myself—that I fully realized that it must have been an uphill battle all the way to get that degree. She persisted through a very long trek: by the time she finished, I was in high school and served as the proofreader for her dissertation.

I will never forget what my mother told me when I became a mom and started struggling with the work-children balance: that children can always tell if you are leaving to escape them or if you are eager to hurry back.

This had a ring of truth to me, because even with all that my mother worked to accomplish when I was young, I cannot remember ever for one moment feeling that I was anything but number one on her list of concerns.

In fact, I have no memory at all of ever being left somewhere. When I started looking into the day care issue as a policy analyst, it suddenly dawned on me that I had no idea what my parents had done with my brother and me when we were little. As it turned out, that's because they worked together as a tag team, coordinating their schedules so that one of them could be with us.

That was typical of their approach to everything. Teamwork. And they always incorporated us into their lives. One of my early memories is of computer cards. I sit writing this book on a computer at home on my desk—I can access worldwide research with the click of a button through the Internet. However, when my parents were students, computers took up whole huge rooms, and researchers had to fill out and feed in keypunch cards to get the information they needed. So we all went together. I can remember hanging out as a small child with my parents, waiting on the computer—my brother and I running around the lobby area playing with the discarded punch cards.

Out behind the university building where my father taught economics and my mother's department had offices, there was a huge field with dirt mounds and cattails growing. Gil and I would wait for our parents and build pretend forts, running free. Those are happy memories—Mom and Dad were busy, but we were a part of it all.

This was all part of my parents' shared vision. When I think of my childhood, I think of common goals: my father supported and encouraged my mom, and she did the same for him. And somehow my brother and I were thrown in the mix as we all worked on the same team.

But it wasn't all work—they made time for the fun, kid stuff. Of course my mom would be the volunteer mother who chaperoned the school field trip. Of course my mom would make my Easter bunny costume for the school play. Somehow, in the midst of doctoral studies, she helped me bake, and ice, several dozen pink, heart-shaped cookies to take to my second-grade Valentine's Day party. I can only remember one time worrying that my dad would be late for a recorder concert of mine. I had a solo. He made it. They both always did.

Growing up, I took it for granted that kids got to spend a lot of time with their parents and go on summer vacations.

But in the midst of all that they were doing, there was a lot they were not doing. I know that now.

I didn't know then that other kid's parents were busy writing and publishing articles in the summertime and working furiously toward tenure all throughout the year. That kind of work doesn't leave a lot of time left over for recorder concerts and field trips. My parents consciously sacrificed to put us first.

So instead of tenure, they opted for a rich and varied life. Those costumes my mom kept creating slowed down her doctoral research, but she got there. And then she went on to a lot of other places: she moved out of teaching and into college administration. She received a National Chamber of Commerce Community Leadership Award and was Woman of the Year. She became a consultant and a writer. Eventually she hit the nation's capital with a bang and became a speechwriter to the secretary of health and human services (remember the culture of character and Healthy Start?) and finally speechwriter to the president.

Even with so much going on in her career, my mom always wanted to know what was happening in her children's lives. Typically, I would call home from college (or wherever) and tell her a long, convoluted story with a full cast of characters. I would say, "You probably don't remember so-and-so . . ."

She would interject, "Sure I do." And she did. Other details she might forget in a busy life. But when it came to the details about her children's lives—people we've known, places we've been—she always remembered.

Maybe that's because she has personally known all the significant friends of mine from every era in my life—she was always The Mom Who Was There. She was the one who drove halfway across the state to be in the stands at the cheerleading competition. Years later she was the one who drove across several states for a weekend blitz to help make the college campaign posters.

Her kids weren't the only ones she sacrificed for. She modeled for me a woman who influenced the larger community through the lives she touched—our home was always open. College students were always coming over for fun get-togethers but also seeking serious guidance about deep life struggles. And there was a steady procession of my (and my brother's) friends congregating at our house. Still today there always seems to be someone staying for short or extended periods in my parents' guest bedroom.

But the most significant—and wrenching—sacrifice to watch was the time my mother opened her home to her mother-in-law. My grandmother was dying of Alzheimer's when my mom put her dining-room table in storage and set up a hospital bed right in the middle of the house in order to take care of Grandma round the clock in her final months.

The only way you could tell what a sacrifice it was, was if you knew Mom well enough to see the fatigue and strain in her eyes. She was trying to hide it, because at the same time, she was helping me plan my wedding.

She's still modeling the balancing act. Blazing the trail of radical motherhood. One day crafting a massive PR campaign about the Beijing Conference. The next day painting my two-year-old daughter's fingernails.

Funny how life comes full circle. My mother was the one who taught me how to write. I remember sitting at her kitchen table with notes for a paper spread out in a jumble. My mother showed me how to cut up the notes into pieces, arrange my thoughts in order, and then tape them together to form my outline. Now, years later, the scissors and tape are icons on a computer screen. And as I write this book, my children are lulled to sleep by the tappity, tappity, tap of a computer keyboard.

I'm still moving words and thoughts around like she taught me. And my mom is still there. Only now it's at *my* kitchen table, where source books are spread all over as she checks my footnotes and straightens out my syntax.

What's this fax coming through?

Charlie:

Did you see this article on moms who take their babies to work? I thought you might want it for the book.

Love, Mom

Deborah's Tribute

My earliest memory of my mother (Charmaine's grand-mother) is our trip to the library for story time. I held her hand as we walked across town. I sat, leaning against her, as we listened to the story. We stopped on the way home at a bakery to buy gingerbread men. We ate our cookies under a tree. When I was with my mama, the skies were blue, birds sang, my world was filled with sunshine and joy.

Another day, as a preschooler, I stood on our front porch, telling my brother and sister something important. But because of my childhood speech impediment, neither of them could understand me. I repeated those words over and over, with a growing lump in my throat. How frustrating that no one could understand me! Then someone ran for Mother and she came out on the porch, listened carefully to what I had to say, and translated for my siblings. Mother always knew what I was saying. And she still knows my heart when others hear only my words or see only my actions.

The most important and influential woman in my life was born Sarah Ruth Baird in 1923, the youngest of eleven, two of whom died as children. She grew up during the hard years of the Depression. Her father, who worked in a textile mill after he gave up the family farm, died when she was only nine years old.

When Mother was fifteen and a half, she married a nineteen-year-old boy from a neighboring town. In the next nineteen years, she and Charles Shaw had seven children: Janice, Joan, Terrell, Carol, Deborah, Beth, and David. She finished high school after her two oldest daughters were born and before my father served in World War II.

When they had four children, Daddy felt called to preach. So Mother packed up the family and set out with her husband on a new adventure—college in another state, away from family and friends. I was their fifth child, born while my father was a college student, before he started seminary.

My parents spent the better part of the next four decades moving and ministering together at several United Methodist churches in cities and towns throughout north Georgia. While Daddy preached, Mama mothered seven children, made do on a preacher's salary, and fulfilled all the responsibilities of a pastor's wife.

I never fully appreciated the personal sacrifices she made or the personal dreams she postponed for so long, until I read the poem she wrote about that time in her life. She titled it:

A Woman's Work Is Never Done

That poem that came .. into my heart
Unexpected ... like a dart
I want to polish ... For discerning.
To write it down, ... Oh, the yearning.

First, I must polish .. Something more.
That spot from off ... the kitchen floor.
What did I write? ... A note that said,
"Excuse my child ... He's sick in bed."

I also write ... some words to note,
Call the dentist ... Hem brown coat.
Wash blue sweater ... Start the roast
Toss a salad ... Bread for toast.

Wash the dishes ... fold the clothes
Sew a blouse ... Buy ribbon bows
Make a poster ... Draw a fish
Prepare another ... covered dish.

Wash the windows ... Doors and sill
Grab the telephone ... pay the bills.
Buy quick oatmeal ... Cream of wheat
Call repair man ... mend a sheet.

Set the table ... Kiss a hurt
Iron a tablecloth ... Blouse and skirt
And other chores ... I list and do
Just little things ... the whole day through.

So I continue ... Blowing noses
And postpone things ... Like Grandma Moses
But thank you, God ... You've done your part
You put a poem ... Within my heart.

Ruth Baird Shaw

It wasn't until I reached junior high school that my mother found time to do what she had always wanted to do. She began going to college: one or two classes at a time, whatever she could fit into the corners of her life as a mother of seven and a minister's wife. In whatever town we moved to, she would go to the nearest college and ask for a class schedule. A course here and a course there, she slowly pursued her own education. Twenty-two years later she received her college diploma. That same year, her two oldest granddaughters (Lyn and Charmaine) graduated, too.

As a child, I had always loved my mama's poems. Once her nest was empty, Mother compiled a program of her poetry which she is often invited to read to community and church organizations and church groups.

After my father retired, he served as a part-time preacher in a small country church outside Atlanta. When he died, the congregation so loved my mother that they asked her if she would finish out the year as their minister. She agreed.

By the time that year ended, she felt called into the ministry herself. The following fall, at the age of sixty-four, she became a full-time seminary student while continuing to pastor that little church. Three years later when she graduated from seminary, she began the two-year process to become an ordained elder of the United Methodist Church.

Some people questioned the point of pursuing that goal at her age.

She usually responded by telling them a story. When she was in her forties, she had wondered if she wasn't too old to be in college courses. Her brother Bill, who was eighteen years older than she was, advised her, "Ruth, you ought to do it now, while you're still young."

And she was still young enough to earn ordained elder status in her church. Mother served for three years as a full-time United Methodist minister, before mandatory retirement. Now a "retired" minister, she's in her third year serving as "part-time" pastor of a small suburban Atlanta congregation that each year asks the bishop to please let her return. She is in constant demand to perform her poetry program or to be a special speaker for different church and civic groups.

I love reading to this day, because my mother always made time to read to us. I value education, because my mother made it such a priority in her own life. I know that God hears me when I pray, because I heard the prayers of my mother for me and for my brothers and sisters. And I know integrity and perseverance, because I've seen them modeled in my mother's life.

My sisters and I never thought of women as the "weaker sex," because we saw the strength of our mother's life. As a mother, she taught us we could grow up to do or be anything we wanted to be. All five of us girls earned master's degrees. One of my sisters has her Ph.D., and a second is now completing her doctorate.

My mother gave me a vision of the potential power of motherhood. And she gave me an understanding of the true meaning of life, as reflected in words of another one of her poems:

The Old Woman in My Future

Someday . . . Somehow . . . Somewhere in time
She's waiting . . . I will see
An old woman ... Time is making
Time is making . . . out of me!

Will she be a sad complainer,
A fretful tenant of the earth?
Or a kind, productive person
Filled with happiness and mirth?

Please be patient . . . God is making
Molding slowly . . . Out of me
A shining portrait . . . He has promised.
Just you wait and see.

He is smoothing out the roughness
Polishing the dreary places
Filling life with joy and gladness
Pouring out His gifts and graces

God remake me . . . in Your image.
I want to like her . . . when I see
That old woman . . . time is making,
Time is making . . . out of me!

Ruth Baird Shaw

———————————

Janice Shaw Crouse. Ruth Baird Shaw. This is our heritage. These are our mothers. They gave us life. Their love, guidance, and examples forever proved to us the value of mothers. Their belief in their daughters gave us confidence and strength to believe that women can and should make a difference in the world. They were and are our first and greatest models of radical motherhood.

The only way we know to thank them is to "rise up and call them blessed" with this tribute. And to live our lives with the hope and the prayer that we may pass on their legacy to the next generations so that our daughters and granddaughters can do the same.

Acknowledgments

Just as people don't just appear full-grown one day, neither do books simply roll off the press and show up on bookstore shelves. Indeed, writing a book is a lot like parenting a child. First it must be conceived, born, nourished and shaped as it develops and grows toward completeness. It demands energy, discipline and incredible amounts of time and attention. And before you're through you find not only your success but your very survival depends on the input and help you receive from both familiar and unexpected sources.

The two of us (Deborah and Charmaine) want to thank all the folks at Zondervan for their belief in this project: Scott Bolinder, our friend and publisher whose support for this book and whose faith in us always encouraged us; John Sloan our editor, whose input and advocacy made it possible to write the book we wanted to write; Robin Schmitt for his copy editing expertise; and Marketing Director Linda Peterson for championing this book from the beginning and helping get the word out.

We'd also like to thank Gregg Lewis for all the roles he played in this project. He was not only the person who proposed we coauthor a book on this topic, he also volunteered to be our agent and found us a publisher. He used his editorial skills to mold our two voices into one, and he cheered us on when we got discouraged and the looming deadlines looked impossible to meet.

And of course we want to thank the dozens of women who generously shared their time and their hearts with us during in-depth interviews and conversations and whose stories and words are shared in these pages. We've changed all their names and in some cases altered minor details about their lives to protect their privacy. But they know who they are and we want them to know they have our deepest gratitude.

And then there are others we each want to acknowledge.

Charmaine

It is humbling to reach the end of a project like this and put my name on it, when every word written represents, in some way, the team effort of so many people who have supported, encouraged, and worked with me. The emphasis in this book on teamwork reflects my own recognition of how important the contribution of others has been in my life. I want to thank those people.

First, my thanks to my co-author, Debi, and her husband, Gregg, our Agent Extraordinaire and unofficial editor/cleaner-upper. This project has produced the synergy that we hoped for and been remarkable conflict-free. Debi, it has been a joy to work together. And Gregg, I appreciate your vision for this book and the energy and skill you poured into making it happen.

I want to thank friends and colleagues who took the time to give feedback on the manuscript (on an amazingly tight deadline) and, in so doing, vastly improved the finished book: Kristi Stone Hamrick, my colleague and friend, was amazingly generous with her time, reading and giving detailed comments and suggestions. She is one of the wisest women I know—she always challenges my thinking, and I feel fortunate that this book reflects some of her insights. Jana Baldwin and Kristin Colber-Baker, my two oldest friends, continuing a long tradition of influencing my life, both took time to read and offered perceptive comments. Thank you to Charles Donovan, from whom I have learned so much over the years; Dr. Brenda Hunter, whose insights led to some important adjustments; and Leslie Nunn, and Kris Napier. And within my family, my brother, Dr. Gilbert Crouse, Jr., and my sister-in-law, Helen

Yoest, both took the time to read, and I deeply appreciate their valuable comments and encouragement.

I want to thank Dr. Steven Rhoads for challenging my thinking and stimulating my interest in the issue of women and work. And for granting me the Bradley Fellowship, which made it possible for me to study at the University of Virginia and begin the research that led to this book.

Thanks also to the friends who encouraged me: Kimberley Lorden and Pam Rogers; Ruth Darling Simpson, and my cousin, Zoe Brown Custer.

There are several people who have made up a personal team for the Yoest household, and to them I owe an enormous debt for all that they did to take up the slack in our lives: first, thank you to Michelle Prunty who, as my assistant and researcher, diligently tracked down resources and information for me and handled many life details for me, keeping this sleep-deprived mother on track. "Selle" became a valued member of our merry little band. Second, thank you to David Crouse III, who also contributed enormously—with gallons of milk, beating a path to Federal Express, and tossing my kids in the air. And third, to Elsie Melgar ... your hard work, unflagging cheer, and love for children are appreciated beyond measure. God sent you to us, and we all love you.

As much as any other story in the pages of this book, I am the mother in the middle. Even while writing about the effort to balance children and work, I struggled on a daily basis. I came away with a deeper realization that accomplishment for a mother requires a deep commitment from those closest to her. This project involved huge sacrifices from the people who love me. The book was completed only with the help and support I got from my family, particularly my parents. I pay tribute in the book to my mother, so let me just say here that she was there for me when the going got tough, even when it interfered with her own life: from the practical details of bringing in dinner and giving my kids baths to professional assistance in editing and research. Thank you, Mom.

264 Mother in the Middle

I cannot adequately express the depth of my indebtedness to my father, Dr. Gilbert Crouse. First, the accuracy of the data in this book is due to his diligence both in finding quality research but also checking and triple-checking my abysmal math. (Any errors, of course, are entirely my own.) And he read and smoothed portions of the manuscript more times than he cares to remember. Second, as I read these pages, I see everywhere his influence: I have learned, and continue to learn, so much from him. Lastly, in researching feminist history and thought, it is difficult to read of the personal pain and disillusionment that has shaped so many women's attitudes toward men and family life. Tragically, they then see themselves through that prism of pain as well. I have been free of that baggage because my father loved me unconditionally and believed in me. The world has broader horizons for me, and I believe in radical motherhood, as a result. That was in immeasurable gift. Thank you, Dad.

I married another man who believes I can do anything . . . even when I don't believe. It is an amazing gift to live with someone who never doubts, whose vision is always clear, and whose support is unflagging. My husband, Jack, is my number one collaborator. He is the one to whom I owe the deepest debt.

And lastly, to Hannah and John . . . you are my joy.

Deborah

I want to thank my research assistant, secretary, sounding-board, and little sister Beth Shaw for her interviewing, research and clerical help on this book.

I need to thank Wendy Williams, Debbie Jones and Liz Trammel for taking up the slack at PALS so I could devote my energies and meet the deadline on this book. I also want to thank the mothers who took the time to read and react to an early draft of the manuscript—Zelda Buford, Karen Tucker, Carol Johnston, Annette Clairy, Regina Threlkeld, Wanda

Hodges, Wendy Williams, Carol Payne, Susan Banks and Joan Turrentine. I also owe a great debt to the hundreds of mothers I've met and talked to over the last few years about the issues of motherhood; they helped shape my thinking and encourage my concern.

Last, and most importantly, I want to thank my family for their patience and understanding. My husband, Gregg, who was not only involved as agent and editor on the book, but also did more than his usual share of cooking, driving, and parenting of our kids when I was at the keyboard. And especially my five children, Andrew, Matthew, Lisette, Benjamin, and Jonathan who have taught me what incredible joy and satisfaction there is in being a mother in the middle.

Endnotes

Prologue

1. Bureau of Labor Statistics, *Handbook of Labor Statistics*, Bulletin 2340 (August 1989) and *Employment and Earnings* (January 1995 and earlier).

2. Ibid.

3. Amitai Etzioni, "Children of the Universe," *Utne Reader* (May/June 1993), 52–61.

Chapter One

1. Marney Rich Keenan, " Mothers' Nature: There Isn't Any Harder Job Than Leaving Baby Behind," *Detroit News* (May 12, 1990), C1+.

2. Arlie Hochschild with Anne Machung, *The Second Shift* (New York: Avon Books, 1989), 3–9.

3. Deborah Shaw Lewis, *Motherhood Stress* (Grand Rapids, Michigan: Zondervan Publishing House, 1989), 111.

4. Abigail Van Buren, "Mom needs a vacation from home," *The Washington Times*, (November 14, 1995), C 11. Distributed by Universal Press Syndicate. Reprinted with permission. All rights reserved.

5. Urie Bronfenbrenner, "Discovering What Families Do," David Blankenhorn, Steven Bayme, Jean Bethke Elshtain, eds., *Rebuilding the Nest: A New Commitment to the American Family* (Milwaukee, Wisconsin: Family Service America, 1990), 31.

6. Mother Teresa, message sent to and read at the Fourth United Nations World Conference on the Rights of Women, August, 1995, in Beijing.

7. Abigail Adams, "Familiar Letters of John Adams and His Wife, Abigail Adams, During the Revolution," Miriam Schneir, ed., *Feminism: The Essential Historical Writings* (New York: Vintage Books, 1972), 3–4.

Chapter Two

1. Mary Wollstonecraft, *A Vindication of the Rights of Woman* (1792), Carol H. Poston, ed. (New York: W. W. Norton, 1988), 151.

2. Deborah Diamond, "The Hardest Job in the World," *Ladies Home Journal* (October 1995), 163.

3. Elizabeth Austin, "6 Mistakes Working Mothers Make," *McCall's* February 1995), 74.

4. Jacqueline Shannon, "Can You Be Somebody and a Mommy Too?" *Cosmopolitan* (October, 1994), 125.

5. Gabrielle Palmer, *The Politics of Breastfeeding* (London:Pandora Press, 1988), 129.

6. Ruth Schwartz Cowan, *More Work for Mother* (New York: Basic Book, 1983), 38.

7. Ibid, 85, 100–101.

8. Claudia Goldin, *Understanding the Gender Gap: an Economic History of American Women* (New York: Oxford University Press, 1990), 43, 12.

9. Betty Friedan, *The Feminine Mystique* (New York: Dell Publishing Group, Inc., 1963), 32.

10. Ibid.

11. Henrik Ibsen, *Four Major Plays*, James McFarlane and Jens Arup, trans., (Oxford: Oxford University Press, 1981), 81–82, viii.

12. *Kramer v. Kramer*—Columbia Pictures, 1979.

Chapter Three

1. Miriam Schneir, ed., *Feminism: The Essential Historical Writings* (New York: Vintage Books, 1972), xvi.

2. Betty Friedan, "Beyond Gender," *Newsweek* (September 4, 1995), 31.

3. Miriam Schneir, ed., *Feminism: The Essential Historical Writings* (New York: Vintage Books, 1972), 82.

4. Ibid, 99.

5. Barbara Ehrenreich, "Strategies of Corporate Women," *The New Republic* (January 27, 1986), 30.

6. Sue Shellenbarger, "Some Workers Find Bosses Don't Share Their Family Values," *The Wall Street Journal* (July 12, 1995), A1.

7. Matthew 19:13–15; Mark 10:13–16; Luke 18:15–17.

8. Anne Dally, *Inventing Motherhood: The Consequences of an Ideal* (New York: Schocken Books, 1983), 105–6.

9. Charlotte Latvala, "Great! Now My Friend's a Mom-to-Be—But is She Still My Friend?" *Cosmopolitan* (September 1993), 162.

10. Carol Lawson, "Don't Let the Guilt Get to You," *Cosmopolitan* (October,1993) 148–50.

11. Paulette Thomas, "United States: Success at a Huge Personal Cost," *The Wall Street Journal* (July 26, 1995), B1.

12. G. K. Chesterton, "Turning Inside Out," *Essays of Our Times*, Sharon Osborne Brown, ed. (1928), 91–2: from *Fancies Versus Fads* (Dodd, Mead and Company, Inc., 1923).

13. Henrik Ibsen, *Four Major Plays* , James McFarlane and Jens Arup, trans. (Oxford: Oxford University Press, 1981), viii.

14. Miriam Schneir, ed., *Feminism: The Essential Historical Writings* (New York: Vintage Books, 1972), xvi.

15. Hal Lancaster, "Two Women Hire Help to Smash the Glass Ceiling," *The Wall Street Journal* (November 14, 1995), B1.

16. Ibid.

17. Wade Lambert, "Women Lawyers Talk About Double Standard At Work, in New Book," *The Wall Street Journal* (October 16, 1995), B5.

18. David Blankenhorn, *Fatherless America: Confronting Our Most Urgent Social Problem* (New York, New York: Basic Books, 1995), 5.

19. "More Women At the Top," *Chief Executive, No. 109* (December 1995), 49.

20. G. K. Chesterton, "Turning Inside Out," *Essays of Our Times*, Sharon Osborne Brown, ed. (1928), 91–2: from *Fancies Versus Fads* (Dodd, Mead and Company, Inc., 1923).

21. Iris Krasnow, "Surrendering to Motherhood," *The Washington Post* (November 22, 1994), D5.

22. Miriam Schneir, ed., *Feminism: The Essential Historical Writings* (New York: Vintage Books, 1972), frontispiece.

Chapter Four

1. Barbara Dafoe Whitehead, "The New Family Values," *Family Affairs* (New York: Institute for American Values, Summer 1992).

2. Dr. Fran Stott, Dean, Erikson Institute, personal conversation with Deborah Shaw Lewis, December 1, 1995.

3. Stanley Greenspan and Nancy Thorndike Greenspan, *The Essential Partnership* (New York:Viking , 1989), 5–6.

4. Erik H. Erikson, *Childhood and Society* (New York: W. W. Norton and Company, 1950), 219–27.

5. Robert Karen, *Becoming Attached: Unfolding the Mystery of the Infant-Mother Bond and Its Impact on Later Life* (New York: Warner Books, 1994), 4.

6. Ibid.

7. Jay Belsky, "Parental and Nonparental Child Care and Children's Socioemotional Development," *Journal of Marriage and the Family* (November 1990), 890.

8. Peter J. LaFreniere, and L. Alan Sroufe, "Profiles of peer competence in the preschool: Interrelations between measure, influence of social ecology, and relation to attachment history," *Developmental Psychology* (1985), 56–69; as cited by Belsky, 890.

9. Virginia L. Colin, "Human Attachment—What We Know Now," *Infant Attachment Literature Review for the U. S. Department of Health and Human Services* (June 28, 1991), 13.

10. Jay Belsky, "Parental and Nonparental Child Care and Children's Socioemotional Development," *Journal of Marriage and the Family* (November 1990), 895.

11. Virginia L. Colin, "Human Attachment—What We Know Now," *Infant Attachment Literature Review for the U. S. Department of Health and Human Services* (June 28, 1991), 119.

12. Virginia L. Colin, *Infant Attachment—What We Know Now, Executive Summary* (Washington: U. S. Department of Health and Human Services, June 28, 1991), 119.

13. Robert Karen, *Becoming Attached: Unfolding the Mystery of the Infant-Mother Bond and Its Impact on Later Life* (New York: Warner Books, 1994), 66.

14. Bernice Kanner, "Mother Love," *New Woman* (May 1991), 69.

15. T. Berry Brazelton, *Touchpoints* (Reading, Massachusetts: Addison-Wesley Publishing Company, 1992), 367–73.

16. Marney Rich Keenan, "Mothers' Nature: There Isn't Any Harder Job Than Leaving Baby Behind," *Detroit News* (May 12, 1990), C1+.

17. Salem Alaton, "What Is He, What is She," *The Globe and Mail* (Toronto, Canada), (August 22, 1992) D1+.

18. Ibid.

19. Heather Pringle, "The Sex Difference," *Equinox* (Camden East, Canada), (Sept./Oct. 1992) 84+.

20. Donald Joy, *Bonding* (Waco, Texas: Word Books, 1985), 122–26.

21. Maria Piers, *Growing Up with Children* (Chicago: Quadrangle Books, 1966), 18.

Chapter Five

1. National Center for Health Statistics, *Vital Statistics of the United States* (1989), Vol. 3; and Marriage and Divorce, *Monthly Vital Statistics Report*, Vol. 42, No. 12 (May 13, 1994).

2. Arlie Hochschild, *The Second Shift* (New York: Avon Books, 1989), 249.

3. Ibid, 251.

Chapter Six

1. Joann S. Lublin, "Some Adult Daughters of 'Supermoms' Plan to Take Another Path," *The Wall Street Journal* (December 28 , 1995), A1.

2. Suzanne Gordon, *Prisoners of Men's Dreams* (Boston: Little, Brown and Company, 1991), 202–203.

3. Ibid, 103.

4. Deborah Fallows, *A Mother's Work* (Boston: Houghton Mifflin, 1985) 126–27.

5. Betty Friedan, *The Feminine Mystique* (New York: Dell Publishing Group, Inc., 1963), 33–68.

6. Suzanne Gordon, *Prisoners of Men's Dreams* (Boston: Little Brown and Company, 1991), 28.

Chapter Seven

1. Charles Leroux and Cindy Schreuder, "Handle with Care: To thrive, newborn babies require a vital touch," *Chicago Tribune* (October 30, 1994), Section 1, 1, 18.

2. Urie Bronfenbrenner, "What Do Families Do?" *Family Affairs* (New York: Institute for American Values, Winter/Spring 1991).

3. Erik H. Erikson, *Childhood and Society* (New York: W. W. Norton and Company, 1950), 219–227.

4. Dorothy Conniff, "Day Care: A Grand and Troubling Social Experiment," *The Progressive* (November 1988).

5. William R. Prosser and Sharon M. McGroder, "The Supply of and Demand for Child Care: Measurement and Analytic Issues," *Child Care in the 1990s: Trends and Consequences*, Alan Booth, ed. (Hillsdale, New Jersey: Lawrence Erlbaum Associates, 1992), 47.

6. "Cost, Quality and Child Outcomes in Child Care Centers," University of Colorado at Denver, the University of California at Los Angeles, The University of North Carolina and Yale Unversity. As quoted in *The Atlanta Constitution* (February 6, 1995).

7. Deborah A. Phillips and Carollee Howes, "Indicators of Quality Child Care: Review of Research," in *Quality in Child Care: What Does Research Tell Us?* Deborah A. Phillips, ed. (Washington: National Association for the Education of Young Children, 1987), 10.

8. Beth Levine, "Day Care Disgrace," *Woman's Day* (April 25, 1995), 144.

9. Suzanne W. Helburn, ed., "Cost, Quality and Child Outcomes in Child Care Centers: A Technical Report," (Denver: Department of Economics, Center for Research on Economic and Social Policy, University of Colorado at Denver, 1995).

10. Dorothy Conniff, "Day Care: A Grand and Troubling Social Experiment," *The Progressive* (November 1988).

11. Harriet Brown, "The Little Day Care Center That Could," *Ms.* (September/October, 1995), 66.

12. Deborah A. Phillips and Carollee Howes, "Indicators of Quality Child Care: Review of Research," in *Quality in Child Care: What Does Research Tell Us?*, Deborah A. Phillips, ed. (Washington: National Association for the Education of Young Children, 1987), 11.

13. Amitai Etzioni, "Children of the Universe", *Utne Reader* (May/June, 1993), 54.

14. Ellen Ross, "New Thoughts on 'the Oldest Vocation': Mothers and Motherhood in Recent Feminist Scholarship," *Signs*, Vol. 20, No. 2, (Winter, 1995), 397.

Chapter Eight

1. Amitai Etzioni, "Children of the Universe," *Utne Reader* (May/June 1993), 52–61.

2. Benjamin Schwartz, et al., "Respiratory Infections In Day Care," (Proceedings of the International Conference on Child Day Care Health) *Pediatrics* (December 1994), 1018.

_____, and, Ellen R. Wald, Nancy Guerra, Carol Byers, "Frequency and Severity of Infections in Day Care: Three Year Follow-up," *Journal of Pediatrics* (1991) 118:509–14.

_____, and, "Risks of Otitis Media in Day Care Setting," *Journal of Family Practice* (March, 1991), 289.

_____, and, Michael Osterhold, "Infectious Deisease in Child Day Care: An Overview," (Proceedings of the International Conference on Child Day Care Health) *Pediatrics* (December 1994), 987(4).

_____, and, "Day Care Baby Blues," *Prevention* (October 1995), 76.

_____, and, Eugene S. Hurwitz, et al, "Risk Of Respiratory Illness Associated With Day Care Attendance: A Nationwide Study," *Pediatrics* (January 1991), 62(8).

_____, David G. Addiss, et al, "The Compliance of Licensed U.S. Child Care Centers With National Health and Safety Performance Standards," *The American Journal of Public Health* (July 1994), 116(4).

3. Larry K. Pickering and Steven L. Soloman, "Daycare Infections: Children at Risk," *Patient Care* (Special issue: Emerging Infectious Diseases), (May 15, 1994) 118.

4. Stephen Thacker, et al, "Infectious Diseases and Injuries in Child daycare," *Journal of the American Medical Association* (October 7, 1992), 1720–26.

5. _____, ". . . And Air Quality in the Winter (high levels of carbon dioxide in daycare centers)" *Child Health Alert* (April 1992), 2.

_____, "Day-Care Health and Injury: Carbon Dioxide Levels; Playground Safety," *Pediatric Report's Child Health Newsletter* (December 1992), 76(1).

6. James G. Dobbins, et al, "The Risks of Cytomegalovirus Transmission is Child Day Care," (Proceedings of the International Conference on Child Day Care Health) *Pediatrics* (December 1994), 1016.

7. Jody R. Murph, et all, "The Occupational Risk of Cytomegalovirus Infection Among Day-care Providers,"*Journal of the American Medical Association* (February 6, 1991), 603–8.

8. Linda A. Randolph, "The Potential Health Benefits of Child Day Care" (Proceedings of the International Conference on Child Day Care Health: Science, Prevention and Practice) *Pediatrics* (December 1994), 1050(3).

9. Sandi Kahn Shelton, "What's Right About Day Care: When kids receive high-quality care, they gain social and intellectual advantages," *Working Mother* (December 1995), 46–51.

10. Kara Corridan, "For Working Moms Who Still Feel Guilty . ." Redbook (August 1995), 147.

11. Susan Faludi, "The Kids are All Right," *Mother Jones* (November 1988).

12. K. Alison Clarke-Stewart, "Predicting Child Development From Child Care Forms and Features: The Chicago Study," *Quality in Child Care:*

What Does Research Tell Us?, Deborah A. Phillips, ed. (Washington: National Association for the Education of Young Children, 1987), 21–40.

13. Ibid.

14. Susan Faludi, "The Kids are All Right," *Mother Jones* (November 1988).

15. Ibid.

16. Ibid.

17. Sandi Kahn Shelton, "What's Right About Day Care: When kids receive high-quality care, they gain social and intellectual advantages," *Working Mother* (December 1995), 46–51.

18. Ibid.

19. Robert Mendelsohn, "The Dangers of Day Care Debated," *The Doctor's People Newsletter* (March 1992), 8.

20. K. Alison Clarke-Stewart, "Predicting Child Development From Child Care Forms and Features: The Chicago Study," *Quality in Child Care: What Does Research Tell Us?*, Deborah A. Phillips, ed. (Washington: National Association for the Education of Young Children, 1987), 21–40.

21. Sandi Kahn Shelton, "What's Right About Day Care: When kids receive high-quality care, they gain social and intellectual advantages," *Working Mother* (December 1995), 46–51.

22. K. Alison Clarke-Stewart, "Predicting Child Development From Child Care Forms and Features: The Chicago Study," *Quality in Child Care: What Does Research Tell Us?*, Deborah A. Phillips, ed. (Washington: National Association for the Education of Young Children, 1987), 21–40.

23. David D. Matson, "Viral Gastroenteritis in Day Care Settings: Epidemiology and new Developments," (Proceedings of the International Conference on Child Day Care Health) *Pediatrics* (December 1994), 999(3).

_____, and, Larry K. Pickering and Steven L. Soloman, "Daycare Infections: Children at Risk," *Patient Care* (Special issue: Emerging Infectious Diseases), (May 15, 1994) 118.

_____, and, Eugene S. Hurwitz, et al, "Risk Of Respiratory Illness Associated With Day Care Attendance: A Nationwide Study," *Pediatrics* (January 1991), 62(8).

24. Hillel Goelman and Alan R. Pence, "Effects of Child Care, Family, and Individual Characteristics on Children's Language Development: The Victoria Day Care Research Project," *Quality in Child Care: What Does Research Tell Us?*, Deborah A. Phillips, ed. (Washington: National Association for the Education of Young Children, 1987), 89–99.

25. *1995 Virginia Slims Opinion Poll: A 25-Year Perspective of Women's Issues* (New York: Roper Starch Worldwide, Inc.), 44.

26. Barbara Ehrenreich, "In Search of a Simpler Life," *Working Woman* (December 1995), 28.

27. Lynne M. Casper, Mary Hawkins, and Martin O'Connell, "Who's Minding the Kids? Child Care Arrangements: Fall, 1991," *Current Population Reports, Household Economic Studies, P70–36*, Bureau of the Census, U. S. Department of Commerce (May 1994), Table C., 7.

28. Barbara Turvett, "The Latchkey Solution," *Good Housekeeping* (October 95), 217–21.

29. Ibid.

30. Amitai Etzioni, "Children of the Universe," *Utne Reader* (May/June, 1993), 59.

Chapter Nine

1. Simone de Beauvoir, *The Second Sex* (New York: Vintage Books, 1989), 513.

2. Sylvia Hewlett, *The Lesser Life* (New York: William Morrow and Company, Inc., 1986), 253–286.

3. Simone de Beauvoir, *The Second Sex* (New York: Vintage Books, 1989), 484–527.

4. Charles Darwin, *The Descent of Man* (New York: P.F. Collier and Son, MCMI), 726.

5. Miriam Schneir, ed., *Feminism: The Essential Historical Writings*, (New York: Vintage Books, 1972), 351.

6. Charles Darwin, *The Descent of Man* (New York: P.F. Collier and Son, MCMI), 726.

7. Glenna Matthews, *Just a Housewife* (New York, New York: Oxford University Press, 1987), 121.

8. Herbert Spencer, *The Study of Sociology* (Ann Arbor, Michigan: The University of Michigan Press, 1969), 341.

9. Lester Frank Ward, *Dynamic Sociology, vol. I* (New York: D. Appleton and Company, 1883), 648.

10. Ibid.

11. Charlotte Perkins Gilman, *Women and Economics* (New York: Harper and Row, 1966), p.180.

12. Ibid.

13. Mary Frances Berry, *The Politics of Parenthood: Child Care, Women's Rights, and the Myth of the Good Mother* (New York: Viking, 1993), 90.

14. Martha Bensley Bruere and Robert W. Bruere, *Increasing Home Efficiency*, (New York: Macmillan, 1914), 177; as quoted by Matthews, 156.

15. Glenna Matthews, *Just a Housewife* (New York, New York: Oxford University Press, 1987), 159.

16. Sylvia Hewlett, *The Lesser Life* (New York: William Morrow and Company, Inc., 1986), 260.

17. John B. Watson, *Psychological Care of Infant and Child* (New York: W. W. Norton and Company, Inc., 1928), 81–82, 87.

18. Mary Frances Berry, *The Politics of Parenthood: Child Care, Women's Rights, and the Myth of the Good Mother* (New York: Viking, 1993), 113.

19. Germaine Greer, *The Female Eunuch*, p. 278 as cited by Ann Dally, *Inventing Motherhood: The Consequences of an Ideal* (New York: Schocken Books, 1982), 174.

20. Betty Friedan, *The Feminine Mystique* (New York: Dell Publishing Group, Inc., 1963), 288.

21. Penelope Leach, *Who Cares?* (Harmondsworth: Penguin, 1979), 40; cited by Ann Dally, *Inventing Motherhood: The Consequences of an Ideal* (New York: Schocken Books, 1983), 179.

22. William Iverson, "Love, Death and the Hubby Image," *Playboy*, (September 1963), 92; cited by Barbara Ehrenreich, *The Hearts of Men: American Dreams and the Flight from Commitment* (New York: Doubleday, 1983), 48.

23. Shulamith Firestone, *The Dialectic of Sex: The Case for Feminist Revolution* (New York: William Morrow and Company, Inc., 1970), 233.

24. Miriam Schneir, ed., *Feminism in Our Time: The Essential Writings, World War II to the Present* (New York: Vintage Books, 1994), 331.

25. Christina Hoff Sommers, *Who Stole Feminism: How Women Have Betrayed Women* (New York: Simon and Schuster, 1994), 22.

26. Ibid, 274.

27. "Sex, Society and the Female Dilemma," (a dialogue between Betty Friedan and Simone deBeauvoir), *Saturday Review* (June 14, 1975), 18.

28. Bureau of Census, *Current Population Reports P60–184*, Money Income of Households, Families and Persons in the United States (1992).

29. Ibid.

30. "Why Women Work," 1990 Virginia Slims Opinion Poll, The Roper Organization, as cited by Brickly Townsend and Kathleen O'Neil, "American Women Get Mad," *American Demographics* (August 1990) 29.

31. *Women: The New Providers* (New York: The Families and Work Institute, 1995), 10.

32. *1995 Virginia Slims Opinion Poll: A 25-Year Perspective of Women's Issues* (New York: Roper Starch Worldwide, Inc.), 44.

33. Barbara Ehrenreich, "In Search of a Simpler Life," *Working Woman* (December 1995), 28.

34. *1995 Virginia Slims Opinion Poll: A 25-Year Perspective of Women's Issues* (New York: Roper Starch Worldwide, Inc.), 45.

35. *Women: The New Providers* (New York: The Families and Work Institute, 1995), 30: "Progress and Pressures," *The Public Pulse* (New York: Roper Starch Worldwide, Inc., September 1995).

36. Julia Wrigley, *Other People's Children* (New York: Basic Books, 1995).

Chapter Ten

1. Antoinette Brown Blackwell, *The Sexes Throughout Nature* (New York: G. P. Putnam's Sons, 1875), 135.

2. Arianna Huffington, "A Blizzard Brings Out the Good," *The Washington Times* (January 16, 1996).

3. Jessie Bernard, *The Future of Motherhood* (New York: The Dial Press, 1974), x.

4. Penelope Leach, *Who Cares?* (Harmondsworth: Penguin, 1979), 125; cited by Ann Dally, *Inventing Motherhood: The Consequences of an Ideal* (New York: Schocken Books, 1983), 325.

5. Jessie Bernard, *The Future of Motherhood* (New York: The Dial Press, 1974). 9.

6. Elizabeth Wayland Barber, *Women's Work: The First 20,000 Years: Women, Cloth and Society in Early Times* (New York: W. W. Norton & Company, 1994), 29.

7. Penelope Leach, *Children First: What our society must do—and is not doing—for our children today* (New York: Alfred A. Knopf, 1994), 20–21.

8. Don Oldenburg, "Kids in the Workplace," *The Washington Post* (December 26, 1995), C5. And, Marianne Kyriakos, "Quality Time With Baby Will on the HIll," *The Washington Post* (September 18, 1995), D1.

9. Oldenburg.

10. Titus 1:5–9.

11. Joan C. Williams, "Deconstructing Gender," *Feminist Jurisprudence: The Difference Debate*, Leslie Friedman-Goldstein, ed. (Lanham, Maryland: Rowman and Littlefield Pulbishers, 1992), 59–65.

12. David M. Blau and Philip K. Robins, "Child Care Demand and Labor Supply of Young Mothers over Time," *Demography* (August 1991), 333.

13. Bureau of Census, Current Population Reports, p60–184, Money, Income of Households, Families and Persons in the United States: 1992.

14. Overview of Entitlement Programs, *The 1994 Green Book*, Table 8, Committee on Ways and Means, U. S. House of Representatives, 103rd Congress, 2nd Session (Washington, D.C.: U. S. Government Printing Office, 1994), 981.

15. Ibid.

16. Ibid.

17. April A. Brayfield, Sharon Gennis Deich and Sandra L. Hofferth, "Caring for Children in Low-Income Families: A Substudy of the National Child Care Survey, 1990," *Urban Institute Report 93–2*, (Washington, D.C.: The Urban Institute Press, 1993), 62.

18. Overview of Entitlement Programs, *The 1994 Green Book*, Table 8, Committee on Ways and Means, U. S. House of Representatives, 103rd Congress, 2nd Session, (Washington, D.C.: U. S. Government Printing Office, 1994), 546.

19. J. K. Lasser, *J. K. Lasser's Your Income Tax, 1995*, (New York: Macmillan, Inc., 1994), 362.

20. Overview of Entitlement Programs, *The 1994 Green Book*, Table 8, Committee on Ways and Means, U. S. House of Representatives, 103rd Congress, 2nd Session, (Washington, D.C.: U. S. Government Printing Office, 1994), 547.

21. Ellen Goodman, "The End of Motherhood As We Knew It," *The Washington Post* (September 16, 1995), A17.

Chapter Eleven

1. Anna Quindlen, "Why I Quit," *Working Woman* (December 1995), 30–33.

2. Ibid.

3. Arlene Rossen Cardozo, *Sequencing* (New York: Collier Books, Macmillan Publishing Company, 1986).

4. Robert Frost, "The Road Not Taken," *The Poetry of Robert Frost*, Edward Connery Lathem, ed. (New York: Henry Holt, 1969).

5. Barbara Ehrenreich, "In Search of a Simpler Life," *Working Woman* (December 1995), 27–29, 62.

Chapter Twelve

1. Barbara Bush, address to Wellesley College graduates, May, 1992.

2. *A Women's World*, Twentieth Century Fox, 1954.

3. Glenna Matthews, *Just a Housewife: the Rise and Fall of Domesticity in America* (New York: Oxford University Press, 1987), 34.

4. Charles Edward Stowe, *The Life of Harriet Beecher Stowe* (Boston and New York: Houghton, Mifflin and Company, 1889), 119–124.

5. Joan D. Hedrick, *Harriet Beecher Stowe: A Life* (New York: Oxford University Press, 1994), 207.

6. Charles Edward Stowe, *The Life of Harriet Beecher Stowe* (Boston and New York: Houghton, Mifflin and Company, 1889), 197–99.

7. Glenna Matthews, *Just a Housewife: the Rise and Fall of Domesticity in America* (New York: Oxford University Press, 1987), 34–35.

8. Proverbs 31:10–31 (NASB).

9. Joann S. Lublin, "Some Adult Daughters of 'Supermoms' Plan to Take Another Path," *The Wall Street Journal* (December 28, 1995), A1.